access English 3

Jill Baker · Clare Constant · David Kitchen

Investigating Words section: Louise Dempsey · Isabel Wright

heinemann.co.uk
✓ Free online support
✓ Useful weblinks
✓ 24 hour online ordering

01865 888080

Contents

Part A: Investigating Literature

1	Exploring poetry	4
2	Exploring story structures	16
3	Exploring language and experience	28
4	Comparing texts	36

Part B: Investigating Non-fiction

5	Choosing formal or informal English	54
6	Making information interesting	64
7	Analysing advice	72
8	Arguing your case	82
9	Persuading readers	90
10	Understanding the influence of media texts	106
11	Explaining your point of view in detail	118
12	Reaching a sensible conclusion	128
13	Preparing for the reading test	140
14	Preparing for the writing test	152
15	Analysing *Macbeth*	162

Part C: Investigating Words

16	Dictionaries and spellcheckers	180
17	Checking your work for spelling errors	182
18	Vowels you can't hear	184
19	Words ending in '-ar', '-er' and '-or'	185
20	Prefixes	186
21	Suffixes: '-able' and '-ible'	187
22	Suffixes: '-en', '-ify', '-ise'	188
23	Unusual plurals	189
24	Word families	190

The following icons are used in this book

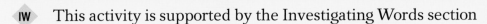

IW This activity is supported by the Investigating Words section

1.1 There is a worksheet to support this activity

1 Exploring poetry

This unit will help you to:
- write poetry
- use different forms of poetry

Advert poetry

This section will help you to:
- write a poem in the form of an advert

1 **Work as a class. Talk together about adverts.**

1 Have you ever bought something from a small advert in a local newspaper? What was it?

2 What sorts of things are for sale in the small adverts in your local paper?

1.1 **2** **Work as a class. Read the poem opposite together. Make sure you understand it. Answer the questions in the labels. Then do the work below to create an advertisement poem with three verses.**

1 Work together on ideas to finish this first verse. Don't worry about making the poem rhyme.

> ### Wanted – a caretaker's assistant
>
> Wanted – a caretaker's assistant.
>
> Must have own set of _____,
>
> And at least one _____ overall.
>
> Needs to _____ piles of litter
>
> And be able to resist the desire
>
> To _____ the students who drop it.

2 Share and write down your answers to these questions.
 a What else might a caretaker's assistant need?
 b What jobs would they do?

Wanted – a witch's cat

1 What does every verse start with?

Wanted – a witch's cat.
Must have vigour and spite,
Be expert at hissing,
And good in a fight,
5   And have balance and **poise**
On a broomstick at night.

Wanted – a witch's cat.
Must have hypnotic eyes
To **tantalize** victims
10   And **mesmerize** spies,
And be an **adept**
At scanning the skies.

2 How many lines are there in each verse?

Wanted – a witch's cat,
With a sly, cunning smile,
15   A knowledge of spells
And a good deal of **guile**,
With a fairly hot temper
And plenty of **bile**.

Wanted – a witch's cat,
20   Who's not afraid to fly,
For a cat with strong nerves
The salary's high
Wanted – a witch's cat;
Only the best need apply.

Shelagh McGee

poise – calmness
tantalize – tease
mesmerize – spellbind
adept – expert
guile – craftiness
bile – temper

Work in pairs.

1 Decide together how you want to finish this second verse.

> Wanted – a caretaker's assistant.
>
> With eyes in ———————————
>
> Who knows how to unblock ——————
>
> Who never panics when ————————
>
> And simply says ——————————
>
> ———————————————

2 Work together on *at least one* more verse for your poem. Look back at your list of what caretakers need and what they do.

> Wanted – a caretaker's assistant.
>
> Must ——————————————

temper?
long hours?
shelves?
keys?
cleaning?

4 **Work on your own. You are going to write your own 'Wanted' poem for a teacher's assistant.**

> **1** Complete this first verse. You don't have to make it rhyme.
>
> > **Wanted – a teacher's assistant**
> >
> > Wanted – a teacher's assistant.
> >
> > Must have amazing _____
> >
> > And a _____ sense of humour
> >
> > Even when _____
> >
> > Needs to be _____ at maths
> >
> > And be able to spell _____
>
> **2** Write *at least one* more verse. Describe the person you would want helping in your classroom. The ideas below may help you.
>
> > Ideas for a teacher's assistant
> > * seven arms
> > * can listen to three people at once
> > * calm
> > * can really talk to you
> > * knows how you feel
> > * doesn't make you feel small

5 **Work as a class.**

> **1** First work in pairs. Read your poems to each other. In each poem, find:
>   * *two* good things
>   * *one* thing that could be improved.
>
> **2** Now share your finished poems with the class. The best verses could be turned into 'Wanted' posters.

Simile poetry

This section will help you to:
- see how another culture uses poetry to describe someone
- write simile poems

Key term

simile – where something is described as **like** something else

1 Work as a class. Read the key term box, then do the work below.

1 Read the sentence in the speech bubble. What do you think it means?

When he opened his mouth it looked **like** the Grand Canyon.

2 Think of some similes you could use to describe someone who is very annoyed.

… like an exploding volcano

… like a thunderstorm

2 Work as a class. Read the poem opposite. Answer the questions around it. Then do the work on page 10.

You!

You!
Your head is like a hollow drum. ——————————— **1** A flat or round head?
You!
Your eyes are like balls of flame.
5 You!
Your ears are like the fans used for blowing fires.—— **2** Small or large ears?
You!
Your nostril is like a mouse's hole.
You!
10 Your mouth is like a mound of mud. ————————— **3** Mouth open or closed?
You!
Your hands are like drum sticks.———————————— **4** Thick or thin hands?
You!
Your belly is like a pot of rotten water.
15 You!
Your legs are like wooden posts. ————————————— **5** Fat legs?
You!
Your backside is like a mountain top.

Based on a traditional Igbo poem from Nigeria

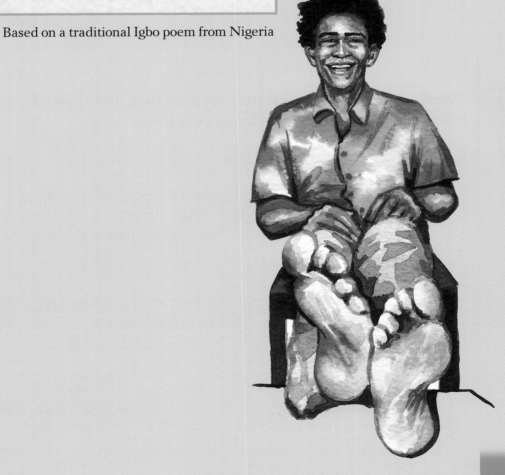

1 Work together on your own 'You!' poem for the person in the picture. Choose the description you think is best to complete each line. Talk about why one description is better than another. Think up some descriptions of your own.

> You!
>
> Your hair is like … — a forest fire
> — a nest for birds
> — a fist of twigs
>
> You!
>
> Your shirt is like … — a tablecloth
> — a summer party
> _____
>
> You!
> Your voice is like …
>
> *loud? roaring?*

3 Work in pairs on the next part of your poem. For these three lines, choose a description or make up your own.

> You!
>
> Your nose is like … — two caves upon the cliff
> — train tunnels
> — a dark path to your head
>
> You!
>
> Your laughter is like … — the start of a sunny day
> — a ringing bell
> _____
>
> You!
> Your teeth are like …
>
> *chalk? a machine for …?*

4 **Work on your own. You are going to write a 'Me!' poem.**

1 Choose the description you think is best to complete this line.

> Me!
>
> My head is like …
> - a box that aches
> - a drawer full of photos
> - a dream machine

2 For these three lines, choose a description or make up your own.

> Me!
>
> My home is like …
> - a bus station in the rush hour
> - a piece of safe ground
> - _____
>
> Me!
>
> My friends are like …
> - a great wave of _____
> - an extra set of arms
> - _____
>
> Me!
>
> My school is like …
> - an ancient _____
> - _____
> - _____

3 Now complete this line with a description of your own.

> Me!
> My room is like _____

4 Try to write *two* more verses. They could be about:
- My eyes
- My life
- My gran
- My mouth.

5 **Work as a class.**

1 Listen to some of your 'You!' poems. Which ones do you like best? Why?

2 Listen to your 'Me!' poems. Which lines work well? Why?

3 If there is time, make a class display of your poems from this unit.

1.3 Riddles

This section will help you to:
- compare different kinds of riddles
- write riddles

1   **Work as a class. You are going to talk about riddles.**

1 A riddle is a description that seems to be nonsense until you know what it describes. Share any riddles that you know.

2 Read the riddle below. It was written in 1893 by the Victorian poet Christina Rossetti. If you cannot work out the answer, look at the picture clues on these pages.

> **A**
>
> There is one that has a head without an eye,
> And there's one that has an eye without a head:
> You may find the answer if you try;
> And when all is said,
> Half the answer hangs upon a thread!
>
> Christina Rossetti

3 Read riddles **B–G**. Try to solve them together. To help you, there are clues all over these pages.

B
To cross the water, I'm the way
For water, I'm above:
I touch it not and, truth to say,
I neither swim nor move.

Anon

C

White bird, featherless,
Floats through the air,
Trees stretch their arms,
The bird settles there.

Anon

D

What has one voice,
With four legs in the morning,
Two legs in the afternoon
And three legs in the evening?

Anon

E

It wears shoes
And runs for miles
But has no feet!

Anon

F

A mouth …
    … but no stomach,
A bed …
    … but no one sleeps there,
A bank …
    … but no one puts money there.

Anon

G

All your strength won't help you much,
For I require the gentle touch;
Turn me and something opens wide
I'm needed most when it's wet outside.

David Kitchen

Work as a class.

1 A riddle is a puzzling description of something that is usually quite ordinary. Riddles can be written in all sorts of patterns. Finish together this riddle about a dentist's surgery.

> A chair …
>
> … but no one _____
>
> A mirror …
>
> … but no one _____
>
> An open mouth …
>
> … but no one _____

2 Which riddle on the previous page had the same pattern as this one?

3 Look back at the patterns of the other riddles. Which riddles have the same patterns as these?

A	**B**
What has …	There is …
With …	You may …
And …	And, when all is …

4 Work together to write a short description of a sport that could be used as a riddle, for example:

> You can find a bar but you won't get a drink,
>
> You'll see a box but you won't open it.   (*Answer: gymnastics*)

This works as a riddle because 'bar' and 'box' each have two meanings.

a Find a word that has two meanings for each of these sports:
   • soccer   • athletics   • snooker

b What other sports do you know that use words with more than one meaning?

c Think of a riddle for one of the sports you have talked about.

   _____ but _____ . (*Answer: _____)*

5 Try writing a puzzling description of what a teacher does.

1.6 **3**   **Work in pairs.**

1 Choose another of the sports you talked about. Use the word you found to make up a riddle.

_____ but _____ .   (*Answer:* _____)

2 Now write a puzzling description of school.

1.6 **4**   **Work on your own.**

1 First write a riddle about one of the sports you have talked about.

2 Now write a puzzling description of a television set.

5   **Work as a class.**

1 Read your riddles to a partner and see if they can find the answers.

2 Choose your best riddles and share them with the class.

3 Put the class's best riddles together on an illustrated wall display with pictures to suggest the answers.

2 Exploring story structures

This unit will help you to:
- look at different ways to begin and end stories
- use different beginnings and endings in your own stories
- write complex sentences to create effects

2.1 Story openings with first- and third-person narrators

This section will help you to:
- look at stories that use first-person and third-person narrators
- write openings that use first-person and third-person narrators

1 Work as a class. First read the key terms box together. Then discuss whether each story starter below uses first-person or third-person narrative.

Key terms

First-person narrative: a story written using a **first-person narrator**. The writer uses 'I' to tell the story. The reader can only know and feel what the main character knows and feels.

Third-person narrative: a story written using a **third-person narrator**. The writer uses 'he', 'she', 'they' or a name to tell the story. The reader is told what is happening to different characters and in different places.

A Sam tore a second page from his exercise book. His homework would never get done …

B I looked out of the castle window and noticed a small cloud of dust in the distance – another knight in shining armour on his way …

C She wore a blue, spotted dress which seemed rather old-fashioned and out of place …

D A rough, aggressive game was not really my kind of thing, but the Bush Street kids were famous for beating their opponents, in every sense of the word …

Work as a class. Read texts A and B below and look at the notes around them. Then discuss these questions.

1 Most stories are written using a third-person narrator. Why do you think this is?

2 Whose view of events does the reader understand when a first-person narrator is used? What might this add to the story?

3 What do you think has happened in story **A**?

4 What do you think is going to happen in story **B**?

1 'I' and 'my' show that this story is told using a **first-person narrator**.

A

Well, I've done it again. No one is surprised, not even my mother who still hopes that one day I might manage to do something right. I am
5 always the kid that gets picked last when teams are chosen; teachers send just about anyone in the class except me on errands, even Joey who is one sandwich short of a
10 packed lunch. No matter how I try, I get everything wrong.

2 A first-person narrator is speaking from inside the story. The reader can only experience the thoughts and feelings of the narrator. The reader only knows what the main character knows.

1 Using a name and 'she' shows that this story is told using a **third-person narrator**.

B

Miss Ronson looked at the table with its silver cutlery and flowers arranged just so. She crossed her arms in the self-satisfied way that
5 she always did when she was pleased with herself. She was unaware of the figure standing at the gate, pausing as if unsure this was the right address. After a few
10 moments, he pushed open the gate and let it shut noisily behind him.

2 A third-person narrator speaks from outside the story, looking in. They can tell the reader what is happening in different places and to different characters. The reader knows more than the characters in the story.

Work with a partner.

1 Read this information about story **B**, then discuss the questions below.

> **Information about story B**
>
> Miss Ronson is Steve Ronson's rich aunt. Steve is poor and is planning to murder Miss Ronson. First, he has to make her write a will leaving everything to him. Miss Ronson lives alone. She hasn't seen Steve since he was a young boy. He is now thirty-three.

a What will Steve and Miss Ronson do when they first meet?

b How will Steve behave towards Miss Ronson?

c What will happen in the next two paragraphs of the story?

2 Now work on your own. Write the next *two* paragraphs of the story. Use the paragraph starter below to help you. Remember:

- Write using third-person narrative. Use words like 'he' and 'she'.
- Describe what both characters do.
- Add details to help the reader imagine what is happening.
- If you include conversation, start a new line when a different person speaks and use the correct punctuation.

> When the doorbell rang, Miss Ronson hurried excitedly to the door. She touched her hair as she passed the hall mirror and then fumbled with the chain on the front door . . .

4 **Work on your own. You are going to write the next *two* paragraphs of story A.**

1 Re-read the beginning of story **A** below. Write down your answers to these questions in note form. Make up what you don't know.

   a Is the narrator a boy or a girl?

   b What has the narrator done?

   c How does the narrator feel about this?

   d What will happen in the next paragraph?

   e What will happen in the second paragraph you write?

   > **A**
   >
   > Well, I've done it again. No one is surprised, not even my mum who still hopes that one day I might manage to do something right. I am always the kid that gets picked last when teams are chosen; teachers send just about anyone in
   > 5   the class except me on errands, even Joey who is one sandwich short of a packed lunch. No matter how I try, I get everything wrong.

2 Now write the next *two* paragraphs of the story, using your notes. You might like to start your paragraph like this:

   > *Take yesterday. I was walking down . . . when I saw . . .*

5 **Work as a class.**

1 First work on your own. Read the two paragraphs you have just written and check that you have:

   • used 'I' and 'my' to show you are writing first-person narrative

   • included only what the narrator sees and does

   • written how your narrator feels about what is happening

   • used capital letters and full stops.

2 Now share your writing with the class. Which did you prefer writing, first-person or third-person narrative?

2.2

Multiple narrators – different views of the same story

This section will help you to:
- explore the use of two narrators in one story
- write part of a story using two narrators

1 **Work as a class. Look at the picture below and discuss these questions.**

1 What might the boy be thinking?
2 How do you think he became homeless?
3 What might the man be thinking?

2

Work as a class. First read the information about *Stone Cold* by Robert Swindells. Then read the extracts and the notes around them. Finally complete these tasks.

1 Which text is narrated by Link and which is narrated by Shelter?

2 Find as many words and phrases as you can which show what Shelter thinks of homeless people.

3 How far is Link to blame for his situation?

4 What does having two narrators add to the story?

Information about *Stone Cold*

Stone Cold is the story of Link, a homeless boy in London, and Shelter, a man who wants to get rid of homeless people. Each character narrates their part in the story separately. The reader experiences the thoughts and feelings of both narrators.

---

1 Both narrators use 'I'.

2 This character used to be in the army so the author has chosen words to show this.

A

I've been out tonight. I took the tube down to Charing Cross and walked about a bit. Tour of inspection, you might say. And I found them, as I'd known I would. Hundreds of the scruffy blighters,
5 lying around making the place look **manky**. I marched along the Strand and there they were, dossing in all the doorways – even Lloyds Bank and the Law Courts.

manky – messy

---

1 The writing style of this text is different to Text A to show it is a different character speaking.

2 The narrator is young so the author has chosen a different writing style to show this.

B

I'd applied for loads of jobs in the months since I'd left school. Office work. Supermarkets. Catering. Filling stations – you name it. Most employers wanted experience, and some ads actually said unemployed
5 persons need not apply, which is criminal, in my opinion. I'd started applying in August and I'd had a couple of interviews, but as I said before, sleeping in your clothes makes you look scruffy, and by Christmas I looked like a tramp. I knew nobody was going to take me on looking like that, and I started getting really depressed.

3 The reader has to piece together the whole story from what both narrators say.

Taken from *Stone Cold* by Robert Swindells

3 Work as a class. You are going to write the next paragraph of the story from Shelter's point of view.

> 1 First read the information in the box below together.
>
> 2 Write *two* sentences of the next paragraph as a class. Make your own copy of the sentences.
>
> 3 Discuss as a class what might come next in the paragraph.
>
> 4 On your own, finish the paragraph. Remember:
>
> - Write as if you are Shelter (use first-person narrative) – use 'I'.
> - Write about the homeless people as if you really hate them.
> - Use unkind words like 'dossers' and 'scruffy blighters' to describe the homeless people.

Information about Shelter

Shelter walks around the London streets looking out for homeless people. He thinks they should all be in the army. He thinks army life would make them better people.

---

4 Work on your own. Write the next paragraph of the story from Link's point of view. In this paragraph Link:

> - describes Christmas on the streets
> - describes begging for money and how cold the weather is
> - says he is lonely and has no money
> - thinks about his family and wonders about the future.
>
> Remember:
>
> - Write as if you are Link (use first-person narrative) – use 'I'.
> - Choose words and phrases that sound like someone speaking.

5 Work as a class.

> 1 Share the paragraphs you have written from Shelter's point of view and from Link's point of view.
>
> 2 Talk about how you have made each narrator sound different.

2.3   Endings – a twist in the tale

This section will help you to:
* explore and write story endings with a twist

1   **Work as a class. First read or listen to the first part of a story below. Then discuss how this story will end.**

Voodoo

Mr Decker's wife had just returned from a trip to Haiti – a trip she had taken alone – to give them a cooling off period before they discussed a divorce.

It hadn't worked. Neither of them had cooled off in the slightest. In
5   fact, they were finding now they hated one another more than ever.

'Half,' said Mrs Decker firmly. 'I'll not settle for anything less than half the money plus half of the property.'

'Ridiculous!' said Mr Decker.

'Is it? I could have it all, you know. And quite easily, too. I studied
10   **voodoo** while in Haiti.'

'Rot!' said Mr Decker.

'It isn't. And you should be glad that I am a good woman for I could kill you quite easily if I wished. I would then have *all* the money and *all* the **real estate**, and without any fear of consequences. A
15   death accomplished by voodoo cannot be distinguished from death by heart failure.'

'Rubbish!' said Mr Decker.

'You think so? I have wax and a hatpin. Do you want to give me a tiny pinch of your hair or a fingernail clipping or two – that's all I
20   need – and let me show you?'

'Nonsense!' said Mr Decker.

'Then why are you afraid to have me try? Since *I* know it works, I'll make you a proposition. If it doesn't kill you, I'll give you a divorce and ask for nothing. If it does, I'll get it all automatically.'

25   'Done!' said Mr Decker. 'Get your wax and hatpin.' He glanced at his fingernails. 'Pretty short. I'll give you a bit of hair.'

voodoo – a kind of witchcraft
real estate – property: land or a house

2

**Work as a class. Read or listen to the ending of the story below.
Look at the notes around the story, then complete these tasks.**

1 Explain the twist in this tale.

2 When does the reader begin to realise there will be a twist in the tale?

3 How does the author stop the reader guessing the twist early in the story?

1 In this paragraph, the reader *assumes* that the hair belongs to Mr Decker. The author doesn't say who the hair belongs to.

30 When he came back with a few short strands of hair in the lid of an aspirin tin, Mrs Decker had already started softening the wax. She kneaded the hair into it, then shaped it into the rough **effigy** of a human being.

'You'll be sorry,' she said, and thrust the hatpin into the chest of the wax figure.

35 Mr Decker was surprised, but he was more pleased than sorry. He had not believed in voodoo, but being a cautious man he never took chances.

Besides, it had always irritated him that his wife so seldom cleaned her hairbrush.

By Frederic Brown

2 Mr Decker behaves in a way the reader does not expect.

3 The twist in the tale – the hair belongs to Mrs Decker.

effigy – small model

2.4 **3** **Work as a class. First read the story idea, then complete the tasks below.**

> ### Idea for a story
>
> It is the year 3002. A class go to the zoo to do some work for their science project. The class need not be made up of humans. The zoo could be on Earth or on another planet. The students walk around the zoo and come across a cage with a new creature in it.

1 Decide where the story is set.

2 Decide whether the people in the class are humans or not.

3 Decide what the new creature in the cage is.

4 Decide what the twist in your tale is going to be.

5 Are you going to give the reader any clues before you reveal the twist in the tale at the end?

6 Are you going to hold back information (for example, whether the students are humans or not)?

7 Write a class plan for the story and put it where everyone can see it.

4 **Work on your own. Write the story from the plan. Remember:**

- Include clues for the reader.
- Let the reader assume some things rather than telling them everything.
- Put a twist at the end of the story.

5 **Work as a class. You are going to check and share your stories.**

1 First work on your own to check your story.
  - Does it make sense?
  - Have you written what you wanted to say?
  - Have you used capital letters and full stops?
  - Have you used speech marks for dialogue?

2 Work in pairs. Ask your partner to check your work for the same things. Make any changes that are needed.

3 Share your work with the class. Say why you are pleased with your story.

2.4 Using complex sentences in stories for effect

This section will help you to:
- use language terms to talk about sentences
- use complex sentences for a particular effect

1 Work as a class.

1 Look at the complex sentence below. A complex sentence contains more than one clause (idea or point). One clause (the **main clause**) gives the main idea or point. The other clause (the **subordinate clause**) adds detail to the main idea.

Although he was late for school	,	Tom stopped to buy some crisps.

This is the subordinate clause. It doesn't make sense on its own.

A comma separates the two clauses.

This is the main clause. It makes sense on its own.

2 Look at the complex sentence below. Decide which is the main clause and which is the subordinate clause.

> While he was running to school, Alan sprained his ankle.

3 A simple sentence only has one clause. Write the complex sentence above as two simple sentences.

2 Work as a class. Read the text below and the notes around it, then do these tasks together.

1 What do the complex sentences help the reader to imagine?

2 Choose one complex sentence. Identify the main clause and the subordinate clause.

1 Simple sentences are used to set the scene. All the still things are described in these simple sentences.

The road was straight. The night was cold. The sky was clear. The moon shone pale. The tall trees by the side of the road cast narrow shadows across it,
5 so that the man who ran, panting and frightened, had the strange impression that he was toiling up a long flight of stairs. … Sweat poured into his eyes, though the night was bitterly cold.

2 The complex sentences which follow describe the running man.

Taken from *Faces* by Dennis Hamley

3   **Work as a class. You are going to rewrite this text using complex sentences. Read the text, then do the work below.**

> Callum ran as fast as he could. He looked over his shoulder. The gang was not there. He could hear them in the distance. Their voices were angry. There were a lot of them. Callum passed the school gate, the gym, the toilets and the staff room. There was no
> 5   one about. He ran. He was hot. He was sweating. His clothes felt heavy. His heart was pounding. He was frightened.

1 Rewrite the first two or three sentences of the text above. Use complex sentences where you think they fit best. You can change words and add anything you think seems right. You could start like this:

> *While he ran as fast as he could, Callum looked over his shoulder.*

2 Now work with a partner. Rewrite the rest of the paragraph. Use a mixture of simple and complex sentences.

3 Work with your partner. Answer these questions to check your paragraph.

   a Read aloud the paragraph you have written. Can the reader imagine Callum running as fast as he can to escape the gang chasing him?

   b Have you used a mixture of simple and complex sentences?

   c In your complex sentences, have you remembered to use commas?

   d Have you used capital letters and full stops?

2.6 **4**   **Work on your own. Write a description of someone falling down a mountainside or some stairs. Remember:**

   • Try to help the reader imagine what falling feels like.

   • Use a mixture of simple and complex sentences to describe falling.

   • Use a comma to separate the main clause and the subordinate clause in a complex sentence.

2.7 **5**   **Now work as a class. Share your descriptions. Pick out good examples of complex sentences.**

3 Exploring language and experience

This unit will help you to:
- compare poems by two poets
- see how experience influences writing
- see different perspectives
- act out a tense scene

3.1 Seeing the influence

This section will help you to:
- talk about the issues and ideas in what you read
- see how a writer's experience influences what they write

1 **Work as a class. Read the information about Jackie Kay, then do the tasks below.**

> **Jackie Kay**
>
> Jackie Kay is a leading black British poet and playwright. Her mother was Scottish and her father was Nigerian. She was adopted by a white couple and grew up in an area of Glasgow where there were few other black people.

1 Talk about what it must have been like to grow up in Jackie Kay's situation.

2 Imagine you looked different in some way from everyone else at primary school. What problems might you have had? How could you have coped with them?

2 **Work as a class. Read the poem by Jackie Kay opposite.**

1 Read the first stanza again and look at the notes together. Say what is happening in *two or three* sentences.

2 Read the second stanza and look at the notes. Say in *two or three* sentences what is happening and how you think the writer feels.

3 **Work in a group of three or four.**

1 Read the third stanza again and look at the notes. Say in *two or three* sentences how the writer would like to behave in school and what she is feeling.

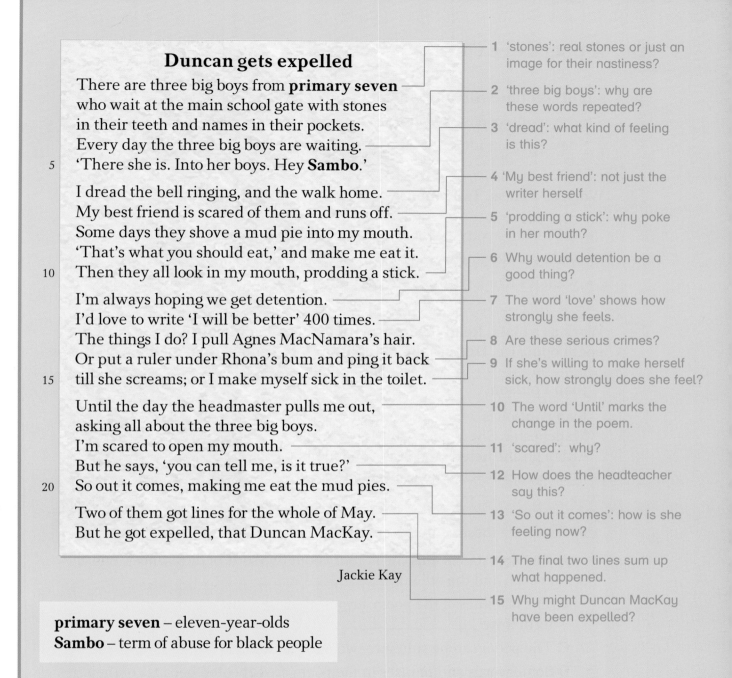

Duncan gets expelled

There are three big boys from **primary seven**
who wait at the main school gate with stones
in their teeth and names in their pockets.
Every day the three big boys are waiting.
5 'There she is. Into her boys. Hey **Sambo**.'

I dread the bell ringing, and the walk home.
My best friend is scared of them and runs off.
Some days they shove a mud pie into my mouth.
'That's what you should eat,' and make me eat it.
10 Then they all look in my mouth, prodding a stick.

I'm always hoping we get detention.
I'd love to write 'I will be better' 400 times.
The things I do? I pull Agnes MacNamara's hair.
Or put a ruler under Rhona's bum and ping it back
15 till she screams; or I make myself sick in the toilet.

Until the day the headmaster pulls me out,
asking all about the three big boys.
I'm scared to open my mouth.
But he says, 'you can tell me, is it true?'
20 So out it comes, making me eat the mud pies.

Two of them got lines for the whole of May.
But he got expelled, that Duncan MacKay.

Jackie Kay

1 'stones': real stones or just an image for their nastiness?

2 'three big boys': why are these words repeated?

3 'dread': what kind of feeling is this?

4 'My best friend': not just the writer herself

5 'prodding a stick': why poke in her mouth?

6 Why would detention be a good thing?

7 The word 'love' shows how strongly she feels.

8 Are these serious crimes?

9 If she's willing to make herself sick, how strongly does she feel?

10 The word 'Until' marks the change in the poem.

11 'scared': why?

12 How does the headteacher say this?

13 'So out it comes': how is she feeling now?

14 The final two lines sum up what happened.

15 Why might Duncan MacKay have been expelled?

primary seven – eleven-year-olds
Sambo – term of abuse for black people

4 **Work on your own.**

1 Read the last two stanzas again and look at the notes. Say in *two or three* sentences what happens and how the writer feels when the headteacher gets involved.

5 **Work as a class. Share your answers about the last three stanzas.**
What issues has the writer made us think about in this poem?
How has she done that?

A poet's eye view

This section will help you to:
- comment on how a writer sees a situation
- develop your ideas through writing about a poem

1 **Work as a class. Talk about:**

- the feelings you get when you start at a new school
- what it's like to start school half way through a year
- what it's like for someone with a different accent to start at a new school.

2 **Work as a class. Read the information about Joan Poulson, then read the poem opposite. Discuss the notes around the poem, then do the work below.**

Joan Poulson

Joan Poulson is white and comes from Manchester. She is now a full-time writer. Although she hated school, she ended up working as a teacher for a short time.

1 Complete these sentences together.

A The first stanza tells the reader about two sorts of differences: one is speech and the other is _____ .

B The last lines of the poem suggest that we will only survive in the long term if we _____ .

C The poem can be split into two parts at line _____ .

D Some words and phrases in the poem are repeated because of their importance. They are _____ and _____ .

3 **Work in pairs. Complete these sentences.**

E The second stanza looks at the differences in _____ .

F The girl's packed lunch is described as 'bizarre'. That is because it seemed _____ to other students.

G The first part of the poem concentrates on the _____ between this new girl and the others.

Different

She was new here and
different; talked different
wore strange clothes

and the food
5   in her packed lunch
     – bizarre!

Everything about her
different
from them.

10   But some of them
     big enough
     to make space for her.

Some big enough to realize
that the world is
15   a place of differences

and that's its richness
the way it was made
– to survive.

1 Note the repeated word 'different'.

2 Strange in what way?

3 Why is food important?

4 What does this mean?

5 Why does this word get a
   line of its own?

6 'But' is a key word – where the
   poem changes.

7 'big' – in size?

8 'make space': what are they doing?

9 Does 'richness' mean money or
   something else?

10 Why do we need to be different
   to survive?

Joan Poulson

4 **Work on your own. Complete these sentences.**

H The second part of the poem from line 10 looks at how it is
_____ to have variety.

I The writer thinks that people who can accept differences are
_____ .

J The poem says that some pupils were able to 'make space' for the
newcomer. This means that they _____ .

3.1 5 **Work as a class.**

1 Share the ways you have completed your sentences.

2 Complete this statement about the poem:

The most important thing about this poem is _____ .

3.3 Making sense of the differences

This section will help you to:
- compare poems by two poets
- comment on how the poets see things
- show how situations and experiences influence writers

1 **Work as a class. Think about the two poems you have read.**

1 Brainstorm what you remember about Jackie Kay and Joan Poulson.

2 Both Jackie Kay and Joan Poulson are writing about the experience of racial prejudice in school. Listen to both poems again. What differences do you notice in how they are written?

Jackie Kay's poem is about …

The poem by Joan Poulson is written …

3.2 2 **Work as a class. You are going to compare the two poems.**

1 Make your own copy of the chart below on a large piece of paper.

'Duncan gets expelled' by Jackie Kay	'Different' by Joan Poulson

2 Look together at each pair of statements below. Decide which poem each statement describes. Add the two statements to your chart.

> A It's a very personal story.
> B It's about someone but it's not very personal.
>
> C It's a story poem, a narrative.
> D It talks about what could be many people's experience.
>
> E The poem splits into two equal parts.
> F The important change comes quite late in the poem.
>
> G The poem is written in the first person.
> H The poem is written in the third person.

3 Work in pairs. Decide together which poem each statement below describes. Add the statements to your chart.

> I The person writing the poem seems to have been through the experience.
>
> J The poem looks at several kinds of differences.
>
> K In this poem the girl is helped by other students.
>
> L In this poem the girl is helped by a teacher.
>
> M The poem does not comment but it shows the reader how awful a situation can be.
>
> N The poem is about changing people's attitudes.

4 Work on your own. Decide which poem each statement below describes. Add the statements to your chart.

> O There's a real sense of fear in this poem.
>
> P This poem is less about fear and more about solutions.
>
> Q The poem shows how a situation can get so bad that someone prefers to get punished than to face it.
>
> R Key words are repeated to drive the message home.
>
> S The poem seems to be written by someone who has seen racism and is against it.
>
> T The poem seems to be written by someone who has suffered racism herself.

3.3 **5** Work as a class. Look back at the charts you have made.

> 1 Decide on *three* important differences between the two poems.
>
> 2 Find *two* things that you think are really good about each poem.

3.4 Building up the tension

This section will help you to:
- make up and act a tense scene

1 Work as a class.

1 What happened in each of the two poems you have been studying?

2 Talk about some reasons why someone can be an outsider. For example:
- they've come from another school
- they look different
- they have different interests
- they've fallen out with their group.

2 Work as a class. You are going to make up and perform a short play about someone who falls out with their group of friends.

1 Read below about the story so far.

> **The story so far**
>
> Sam and Chris used to belong to the same group of friends. However, there's been a quarrel and now nobody speaks to Chris. Chris is sitting alone after school when Sam comes up.

2 Now listen while two members of the class act out this script.

SAM: What's up?

CHRIS: You know what's up. Everyone's ignoring me.

SAM: That's not true.

CHRIS: When did you last talk to me?

SAM: Err … well I guess it was … I'm not sure.

CHRIS: You see.

SAM: I suppose I do. Still, you didn't have to say what you did to Jay.

CHRIS: I didn't start it …

3   **Work in pairs on your own script. First decide who is going to play each part.**

> **1**   Decide why Sam and Chris have fallen out.
>
> ↓
>
> **2**   Decide how each of them might feel.
>
> ↓
>
> **3**   Act out the situation. Build up tension, then come to a solution.
>
> ↓
>
> **4**   Try to make your play three or four minutes long. If your scene is over very quickly, talk about what you could add in a second version.
>
> ↓
>
> **5**   Act out the scene several more times until it works really well.

4   **Work with another pair. Perform your plays for each other.**

1   Look for *two* good things in each play.

2   Look for *two* things to improve each play.

3   Agree which play should be shown to the whole class.

5   **Work as a class. Show each other some of the plays you have developed.**

1   Say what has worked well in each play.

2   Discuss the problems you had to overcome to make the short plays work.

4 Comparing texts

This unit will help you to:
• recognise meaning in words
• compare stories
• develop what you write about stories

4.1 Reading a story

This section will help you to:
• recognise that words can mean more than you first think
• discuss and share ideas about a story

1 Work as a class. You are going to read a story set in the future. The story was written in 1990 and is told through two telephone calls. First talk about:

• the differences between talking to someone on the telephone and seeing them face to face

• what you would want to say in a telephone call if you hadn't seen your family for a long time.

2 Work as a class. Read this story, then do the work on page 42.

Dad, Can I Come Home?

'Dad? Dad! It's Eve. How are you? What are you doing with yourself? Are you all right?'

'Eve? Eve darling, how are you? It's so good to hear your voice. Where are you? Why can't I see you?'

5 'Dad, the screen of this video-phone isn't working. And the fleet's just returned to Tdir-ah so the queues to use the phones are *ginormous*. It was use this phone or wait another week to find a phone with a working screen.'

'No, no, it's enough just hearing your voice, bunny. Are
10 you all right?'

'I'm fine, Dad.' Eve smiled again, stretching out a **tentative** arm to the blank screen before her. 'I've missed you so much. I just can't wait to get home.'

'So the reports are true? The war *is* finally over?'

15 'The war's over. The treaty was **ratified** three days ago. I should be home within the week, if the shuttle bus doesn't give up under the strain.'

'Bunny, that's great news. Wait till I tell Joe and Luke, and especially Morgan – eh!'

20 Eve's cheeks burned. 'Dad, stop teasing! Besides, Morgan is probably married with eight kids by now.'

'Of course he's not married. He's waiting for you. Mind you, if you told him that, he'd laugh in your face but it's the truth.'

25 'Is it, Dad? Is it really?'

''Course it is.'

'Listen, Dad, I can't stay on the phone for much longer, There's a time limit on all **comms** to Earth until further notice. I … I wanted to ask you for a favour though.'

30 'Go ahead, bunny.'

Eve swallowed hard. 'You've met Janice my co-pilot. Did you like her?'

'Yes, of course I did.' Eve heard the surprise in her father's voice. She ran her dry tongue over her lips.

35 'It's just that … well, we were shot down over Zitunm …'

tentative – uncertain
ratified – agreed
comms – communications

'WHAT! You didn't tell me that … are you sure you're …'

'I'm fine,' Eve interrupted. 'But Janice … but Janice isn't, Dad. She was thrown clear but she went back to get me. She saved my life.'

'So what's the matter with her?'

40 'She … she was shot dragging me clear. Shot with a senso-blaster.'

'Oh no …'

'Exactly, she's lost an arm and both of her legs and her face is severely burnt – almost beyond recognition. And she's not **eligible** for artificial limbs because she broke the rules by going back for me. I

45 know those artificial limbs aren't much use but at least they're better than the nothing she's going to get because of me.'

'Oh my God. That poor, poor kid.'

Silence.

'Eve? What's the matter, bunny?'

50 'Sorry, Dad, I was just thinking.' Eve forced herself to continue, 'Janice smiles a lot but deep down she feels very scared, and very alone. She has no family – no one to go back to. So I said that she could stay with us.'

'Stay with us? For how long?'

55 'For good.'

Eve listened to the silence that filled the video-phone booth. The unspoken plea **reverberating** through her mind deafened her.

'Eve darling, maybe Janice can stay for a day or two, or perhaps even a week, but no way can she live with us permanently.'

60 'Why not?'

'Eve, use your head. I'll always be grateful to Janice for saving your life. Always. But we have to face the facts. Janice is a cripple … she'll need a lot of time and attention. She'll require a lot of care, not to mention money. Our home is too small to have her here permanently

65 and it would cost too much to adapt it.'

'But, Dad, she saved my life. Couldn't we at least try? She wouldn't be too much trouble …'

'Yes she would, darling. Don't you think I'd love to say yes but I can't. Maybe she could go into a hospital for the war wounded and we could

70 visit her?'

eligible – suitable, qualified
reverberating – echoing

'She'd hate that. *Please*, Dad …'

'I'm sorry, bunny, but the answer is no.'

'But I've already told her she could live with us.'

'Then you'll just have to untell her.'

75 'Couldn't we just try, Dad. *Please*, for me?'

'No, Eve. She saved your life and I'll always – *always* be grateful for that but she'd be too much of a burden.'

'Burden?' Eve whispered.

'I'm sorry, Eve.'

80 Silence.

'Come on, Eve. Let's not argue. I haven't spoken to you in over two years. Tell me all about …'

'I can't, Dad. My time's up now.'

'Already?'

85 ''Fraid so. I'll see you soon. Bye, Dad. I love you.'

'I love you too, bunny. I'm going to give you such a homecoming. And Eve. I'm sorry about Janice, but you do understand …?'

'I understand, Dad. Bye.'

'Bye, darling. See you soon.'

90 Eve switched off the video-phone. She stared up at the peeling, **dingy** grey paint on the ceiling of the booth … and cried.

Take a break

- What has happened so far?
- What do you think might happen next?

dingy – dirty

'Mr Walker, it's Janice Sonderguard here.'

'Janice? Well, hello, Janice. How are you?'

'I'm all right, Mr Walker.' Janice studied the image of Eve's father on
the phone. He was just as she remembered, his hair grey at his **temples**
but **jet** everywhere else. A neat, trim moustache and his skin the colour
of oak, his body as sturdy as oak. And smiling eyes. A man you
instinctively trusted. Solid, dependable. Only he was frowning now.

'Why, Janice, Eve told me that you'd lost an arm and your legs. Have
the rules been relaxed? Have you received replacements after all?'
Janice turned away from the screen, her lips a tight, bitter line. It didn't
matter what the politicians and the diplomats said, the war wasn't over
… not by *any* means.

'Congratulations. Eve must be so pleased for you.'

Janice turned back to the screen, staring at Mr Walker's broad grin.

'Mr Walker, *please*.' Janice hugged her arms around her body before
dropping them to her sides. 'Mr Walker, please prepare yourself. I …
I've got some bad news.'

'Eve,' Mr Walker said immediately. 'What's wrong? Has something
happened to Eve?'

'Mr Walker, I don't know how to say this. Eve … Eve committed suicide
this morning. I … I …' The man and woman stared at each other.

'Eve …?' Mr Walker whispered. 'She didn't … she wouldn't … What
are you talking about?'

'*Please*, Mr Walker, I'm telling you the truth. She's dead,' Janice
shouted back. 'She's dead,' she whispered.

'But why? WHY? I don't understand.' Janice jumped as Mr Walker
punched the screen. 'Why are you doing this to me? Why?'

'Mr Walker, Eve spoke to you last night. Did you see her? What did she
talk about?'

'What …?' Mr Walker shook his head slowly, utterly bewildered now,
utterly lost. 'I can't … I … never saw her yesterday. The screen in the
video-booth wasn't working … She talked about you, she wanted you to
stay with us.'

'Me?' Janice said slowly.

temples – sides of the forehead
jet – black

'She told me that you'd lost an arm and both legs– .'

'Oh I see,' Janice whispered.

'I don't understand,' Mr Walker pleaded.

'Eve left you a letter. Can I read it to you?'

130 Mr Walker nodded slowly.

Janice removed the letter from her overall pocket. There was sand in her throat, threatening to choke her as she began to read:

Sorry Dad. I love you. You've explained everything to me very carefully and I think this is the best solution for everyone.

135 'What does that mean?' Mr Walker interrupted. 'Eve *can't* be dead ... I don't believe it.'

'Mr Walker, let me show you Eve. She's ... in the **morgue**. I can transmit the image to you.'

'I don't understand any of this ...'

140 Janice keyed the necessary commands into the console beside the video-phone and the morgue appeared without warning, filled to overflowing with row upon row of body capsules. Janice began to key in the commands to home in on the appropriate capsule.

'Mr Walker, did Eve tell you about our crash on Zitunm?'

145 'Yes, she told me how you saved her life.'

'I didn't save *her* life, Mr Walker,' Janice said quietly. 'It was the other way around. She came back for me ...'

A new image filled the screen now. There in her capsule lay Eve Walker, Captain of the SAXICON ship, with no legs and only one arm

150 and a badly scarred, almost unrecognisable face.

By Malorie Blackman

morgue – a place where dead bodies are held

1 The story is in two parts. In the first part Eve is speaking to her dad. In the second part Janice is speaking to Eve's dad. Look at these comments about the *second* part of the story.

  a How far do you agree with each of the comments?

  b Which *two* comments get to the heart of the story best? Why?

> **A** Eve's dad is very polite. Janice thinks of him as solid and dependable. That's what makes it even sadder.

> **B** When Janice tells Eve's dad what actually happened, he can't believe it. The truth is kept from him until the video picture at the very last moment.

> **C** This is a story about a father who kills his own daughter by what he says.

> **D** The title 'Dad, Can I Come Home?' doesn't make good sense at the start of the story. By the end, it makes perfect sense.

2 Copy and complete these sentences.

  a Eve's dad is confused when Janice phones because _____

  _____

  b At the end, Eve's dad must feel _____

  _____

3 **Work in pairs.**

1 Look together at these four comments about Eve.

   a How far do you agree with each of them?

   b Which *two* get to the heart of the story best? Why?

> **E** Eve is afraid, very afraid. There are all sorts of little clues. When she gets to the tricky part of her call to her dad it says: 'She ran her dry tongue over her lips.'

> **F** Eve has got confused. That's why she gets it all wrong when she speaks to her dad.

> **G** Eve says: 'I just can't wait to get home.' That's only partly true. She really wants to come home but she's scared about how her father will react.

> **H** Eve wants to find out how her dad might cope with her disabilities. He gives himself away when he uses the word 'cripple'. That sounds so negative. He doesn't know that he's describing his own daughter.

2 Copy and complete these sentences.

   a Eve is nervous when she talks to her dad because

   _____

   b Eve tells her dad the story about Janice getting hurt because

   _____

4 **Work on your own.**

1 Look at these four comments about the story.

  a How far do you agree with each one?

  b Which *two* get to the heart of the story best? Why?

> **I** The bit about how Morgan is still not married and still waiting for her seems especially sad when you look back. At that moment in the story we simply think that Eve is coming home. We don't know about her injuries.

> **J** The word that drives Eve to suicide is 'burden'. When her dad says that an injured Janice would be 'too much of a burden' Eve repeats the word. In fact she whispers it as if she can't quite say it aloud.

> **K** The story shows you that it's no good saying you care if you can't prove it.

> **L** It's like a test. Eve is testing her dad. He fails.

2 Copy and complete these sentences.

  a I think that Eve kills herself because _____ .

  b Another title for this story could be _____ .

4.1 **5** **Work as a class.**

1 Talk about which comments you chose in activities **3** and **4**.

2 Share your completed sentences from activities **3** and **4**.

3 Work together to produce the best possible versions of those sentences.

4 Talk about what you think this story has to tell parents.

4.2

Reading an older story

This section will help you to:
- see how language has changed over time
- develop your reading skills
- develop your ideas through writing

1 Work as a class. In *Dad, Can I Come Home?*, characters experienced different fears:

- fear of having to tell someone about a death
- fear of coming home badly injured.

1 Who experienced each of these fears?

2 Who do you think was most afraid?

3 How do you think the father felt?

2 Work as a class. The story below was written by H. G. Wells in 1896. It is about a different kind of fear. Read the story and talk about the notes that show how language has changed since Victorian times. Then do the work at the end of the story.

The Red Room

'I can promise you,' said I, 'that it will take a very tangible ghost to frighten me.' And I stood up before the fire with my glass in my hand.

'It is your own choosing,' said the man with the **withered**
5   arm.

'If,' said I, 'you will show me to this haunted room of yours, I will make myself comfortable there.'

The old man jerked his head back so suddenly that it startled me. 'Are you really going?'

10   'It is what I came for.'

The door to the red room and the steps up to it were in a shadowy corner. I moved my candle from side to side in order to see clearly.

I entered, closed the door behind me at once, turned the
15   key I found in the lock, and stood with the candle viewing

1 Today we would probably say 'real'.

2 Today we would say, 'It's your choice.'

withered – shrunken

the scene: the great red room of Lorraine Castle, in which the young duke had died. Or rather in which he had begun dying, for he had opened the door and fallen headlong down the steps.

20 I began to walk about the room. I pulled up the blinds and examined the windows, leant forward and looked up the blackness of the wide chimney and tapped the dark oak panelling for any secret opening. The fire was laid – and I lit it. When it was burning well, I stood with my back to it and looked at the room again. I had pulled up an armchair and a table, to form a kind of
25 barricade before me, and on this lay my revolver. I felt that nothing supernatural could happen.

The reds and blacks of the room troubled me; even with seven candles the place was dim. I recalled the candles I had seen in the passage. Carrying a candle and leaving the door open, I returned
30 with as many as ten. These I lit and placed where the shadows lay deepest. The room was now quite bright. There was something very cheery and reassuring in those little flames.

It was after midnight that the candle in the corner suddenly went out. Taking the matches from the table, I walked across the room
35 to relight it. My first match would not strike and as I succeeded

3 Today we would say, 'I lit these'.

with the second, something happened. Two candles on the little table by the fireplace went out. I walked back, relit one and, as I did so, saw one of the candles by the mirrors go out, then another. There was no mistake about it. The flames vanished, as if the
40 wicks had been nipped suddenly between a finger and a thumb.

'This won't do!' said I, and first one and then another candle on the shelf followed.

4 Modern version would be, 'I said'.

'What's up?' I cried. At that the candle on the wardrobe went out.

My hands now trembled as I tried to relight the candles. I seemed
45 to be succeeding when four lights vanished at once in different corners of the room. As I stood undecided, an invisible hand seemed to sweep out the two candles on the table. With a cry of terror, I dashed to the corner and then to the window, relighting three as two more vanished. It was like a ragged stormcloud
50 sweeping out the stars.

I was now almost frantic with the horror of the coming darkness. I bruised myself on the table, I sent a chair headlong, I stumbled and fell. But there was light still in the room, a red light. The fire! I turned to where the flames were still dancing, made two steps
55 towards them and the flames vanished.

Darkness closed about me like the shutting of an eye. I flung out my arms in an effort to thrust the blackness away from me, and, lifting up my voice, screamed with all my might. I think I must have staggered to my feet. I know I thought suddenly of the
60 moonlit corridor and, with my arms over my face, made a run for the door.

But I had forgotten the position of the door and struck myself heavily against the corner of the bed. I have a vague memory of battering myself in the darkness as I darted to and fro, of a heavy
65 blow on the head and a horrible feeling of falling.

I opened my eyes in daylight. My head was roughly bandaged, and the man with the withered arm was watching my face. I looked about me, trying to remember what had happened.

'Where am I?' I asked.

IW
p.184

70 They told me then of the red room. 'We found you at dawn,' said he, 'and there was blood on your forehead and lips. You believe now that the room is haunted?'

'Yes.'

'And you have seen it. And we, who have lived here all our lives,
75 have never set eyes upon it. Because we have never dared ... Tell us, is it truly the old earl who –'

'No,' said I; 'it is not.'

'Well?'

'It is the worst of all things that haunt us and that is – *Fear!* Fear
80 that will not have light or sound, that deafens and darkens and overwhelms. It followed me through the corridor, it fought against me in the room.'

'That is it,' said he . 'I knew that was it. A power of darkness. It lurks there always. You can feel it in the daytime, even of a bright
85 summer's day. There is Fear in that room – black Fear – and there will be so long as this house endures.'

5 Modern version would be, 'he said'.

Adapted from *The Red Room* by H. G. Wells

1 How does the narrator sound at the start of the story? Work together to choose your top *three* words from this list: *confident, determined, keen, uncertain, big-headed, organised.*

2 Re-read lines 1 to 50 of the story together. Discuss how you know that the narrator begins to feel nervous. Use the following quotations to help you complete written answers. The first one has been done for you.

A 'The old man jerked his head back so suddenly ...' (lines 8–9)

> The old man jerks his head back and _____ him, but only for a moment.

> The narrator is startled by the old man, but only for a moment.

B 'The reds and blacks of the room ...' (line 27)

> The colours in the room ...

> The colours of the room 'troubled' the narrator ...

C 'My hands now ...' (line 44)

> When a candle ...: he is
> not ... but when a second ...

D 'With a cry of ...' (line 47)

> As the light of the candles
> starts to ... he becomes ...

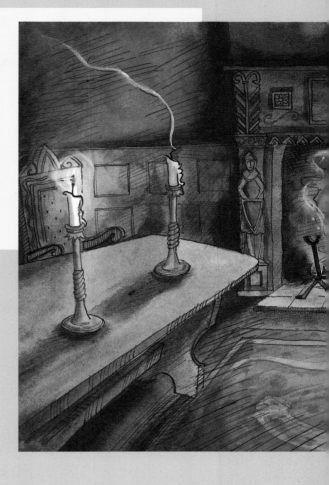

 3 **Work in pairs.**

1 How does the narrator sound by the end of line 55? Choose your top *three* words or phrases from the box.

worried	scared	in a panic
terrified	a bit nervous	still in control

2 Read lines 51 to 65 again. Discuss how the narrator becomes increasingly frightened. Write a paragraph together using information in the quotes below. You could start like this:

> The narrator becomes more and more frightened when ...

E 'I was now almost frantic ...' (line 51)

F 'I flung out my arms in an effort ...' (lines 57–58)

G 'I know I thought suddenly of the moonlit corridor ...' (lines 59–61)

H 'I have a vague memory of ...' (lines 63–65)

Work on your own.

1 Re-read lines 66 to the end. How do you think the narrator feels in the morning? Choose your top *three* words or phrases from the box.

older	foolish	still very scared
relieved	wiser	aware of his weaknesses

2 Copy and complete these sentences.

I When the writer wakes up in the morning, he has a
_____ on his head and the man with the
_____ arm is _____ .

J The man tells him how he was found _____ with
_____ .

K The man wants to know if he now _____
_____ .

L The writer says that the room is not haunted by _____
but by _____ .

5 **Work as a class.**

1 Talk about both sets of top three words or phrases. Agree a class list for each set.

2 Share your sentences from activities **3** and **4**.

3 Do you think anyone will go back into the red room?

4 What do you think the story is trying to tell us?

4.3 | Comparing stories

This section will help you to:
- compare two stories
- compare writers from different times

1 | **Work as a class. Talk about the two stories you have read.**

> **1** Decide *three* important things you could say about *Dad, Can I Come Home?*
>
> **2** Decide *three* important things you could say about *The Red Room.*

2 | **Work as a class. You are going to compare the two stories you have read.**

> **1** Make a copy each of the chart below.

Dad, Can I Come Home? first published in 1990	*The Red Room,* first published in 1896

> **2** Another class collected lots of comments about these two stories, but they got mixed up. Work together to decide which column each comment should go in.

> **A** Words are not always in the order that we would use today.
>
> **B** It's written in the sort of language we use.

> **C** You get little hints about how people are feeling but the story does not tell you much directly.
>
> **D** You know how the main character is feeling because he tells you.

> **E** The writer keeps you reading by gradually building up the sense of fear.
>
> **F** The writer keeps you reading because you can't work out what has happened until right at the end.

3 Work in pairs. Read the comments below.

1 Decide together which column each comment goes in. Put it in your own chart.

2 Talk about *one* thing you could say yourselves about each story.

> **G** The main focus of the story is one person.
>
> **H** The story involves several people who are all important to it.

> **I** You have to work out what has been happening from the conversations.
>
> **J** The writer makes clear what is happening.

> **K** The story is fast moving. Not much is explained until the end.
>
> **L** The story builds slowly and steadily.

4 Work on your own.

1 Read the pairs of comments below. Put each comment in the correct column of your chart.

2 Write a paragraph about each story to sum up what you now know about it.

> **M** Most of the story is told by one person.
>
> **N** The story is nearly all conversation. It's a bit like a mini-play.

> **O** We have a good idea at the end about how things have finished.
>
> **P** We do not know quite how people feel at the end of the story or what they will do next.

> **Q** The message is there in the story but you are expected to work out what it is.
>
> **R** The story tells you at the end what you can learn from what has happened.

5 Work as a class.

1 Talk about which comments fit each story best.

2 Share your paragraphs about the two stories.

3 Talk about which story you enjoyed most. Try to give reasons to back up your choice.

> I liked
> *The Red Room*
> because it made
> me feel ...

> *Dad, Can
> I Come Home?*
> made me think
> about ...

5 Choosing formal or informal English

This unit will help you to:
- listen for bias
- interview people using planned questions
- choose whether to write formal or informal English

5.1 Interviewing to obtain information

This section will help you to:
- use planned questions to interview someone about a robbery
- get extra information by asking follow-up questions

1 Work as a class. You are going to answer questions about the scene in the picture.

1 First work on your own. Look at the pictures below for 30 seconds. Try to remember as much as you can about the crime scene.

2 Now close the book. Discuss as a class what you remember about the scene.

A

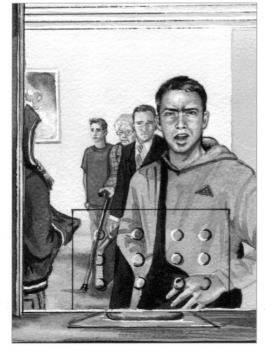

B

5.1 2 Work as a class. The robbers escaped and the police want to questi witnesses. Read the transcript of the interview with the cashier be Look at the notes around it, then answer these questions.

1 What other questions might the police officer ask?

2 Why does the police officer need very detailed answers from the

3 Why might the cashier give too little detail at first in her answers?

POLICE OFFICER:	Were the robbers men or women?	1 This is the question the police officer planned before he arrived.
CASHIER:	Well, I think they were both men but one was very young or a woman. It was hard to tell because the one with the gun turned around and looked the other way.	
		2 The cashier doesn't give quite enough detail.
POLICE OFFICER:	What was it that made you think the second robber might be a woman?	3 This is a **follow-up question** in response to the cashier's answer. It helps her to be more precise.
CASHIER:	He or she had blond plaits poking out from under the hood of their sweatshirt. Blokes don't often have plaits, do they? Also he or she was small and very slim – seems more likely to have been a girl to me.	4 The cashier then explains in more detail.

(line numbers: 5, 10, 15, 20)

3 Work with a partner. You are going to ask some more questions.

1 Write *four* more questions for the police officer to ask the cashier.

2 Role play the rest of the interview using your questions. Take it in turns to be the cashier and the police officer. Ask *two* of the questions each. Then ask follow-up questions to get as much information as possible from the cashier.

Work with the same partner. You are going to role play the police interview with the businessman.

1 Plan and write down at least *five* questions for the police officer to ask the businessman. Use words like *when, where, who, what* and *how*.

2 Now role play the interview. Take it in turns to play the police officer and the businessman.

If you are the police officer

- You must ask the businessman questions to get detailed information about the scene of the crime. You will need lots of detail to find the robbers and then convict them in court.
- The businessman is in a state of shock. He will need a lot of prompting with extra questions to get the detailed answers you need.

If you are the businessman

- You can look at picture **B** on page 54 for 30 seconds before the interview begins.
- Remember that you are in a state of shock – you will find it difficult to answer the police officer's questions.

5.2 **5** Work as a class. Watch some of the role plays the class has worked on.

1 As you watch each role play, make a mental note of when the police officer asks good follow-up questions.

2 After each role play, give the person playing the police officer examples of their good follow-up questions and explain why they were good.

5.2 Changing informal notes to formal reports

This section will help you to:
- write informal notes and turn them into formal reports
- remember how to use quotation marks correctly

1 **Work as a class. You are going to see how well you can use quotation marks.**

    1 Look at the sentences below. Explain why each pair of quotation marks has been used.

> **A** The holiday brochure said the view from the hotel was 'spectacular'. This 'spectacular' view comprised a construction site, an electricity pylon and a bus station.

> **B** The writer uses the phrase 'pools of water in the corners of her eyes' to show that the character is unhappy.

> **C** 'I know who committed the robbery,' said the cashier.

    2 Put quotation marks in the correct places in the sentences below.

> **D** The author creates a tense atmosphere by using phrases like drumming his fingers on the desk and pacing the room like a caged tiger.

> **E** The very efficient bank clerk forgot to count the ten-pound notes.

    3 You have been asked to explain to a Year 8 class how to use quotation marks. Work together to write some rules to help them.

2 **Work as a class. Read the interview notes and report opposite. Look at the notes around them, then complete these tasks.**

    1 What is the purpose of each of these texts?

    2 Find examples of formal and informal vocabulary.

    3 Why is it important for someone who is writing for a court to use formal, standard English?

A

1 The audience for this piece is the police officer who wrote it, so the style is very informal.

2 The notes are not written in full sentences.

3 Verbs and the word 'the' are often omitted.

> Notes from cashier's interview
> Cashier – Helen Bedworth
> Robbery – Southern Bank, Lisle St 20.9.02
> 12.25pm.
> 5 Thinks robbers both men – but one could
> be woman or young girl – plaits poking
> out of s/shirt hood, slim build.
> This one holding gun.
> Man said 'Gimme all the money in the till!'
> 10 Other one pointed gun at customers.
> Both youngish, late 20s at most. One
> asking for money – deep, gruff voice.
> Other one didn't speak.

4 Abbreviations are used.

5 The bank robber's speech is in quotation marks.

B

1 The audience for this report is a criminal court, so the style is very formal.

2 Vocabulary is formal: 'protruding' is a formal way of saying 'sticking out'.

3 Words are written out in full.

INCIDENT REPORT

Robbery at Southern Bank, Lisle Street, London EC14

On 20th September 2002, Southern Bank on Lisle Street was robbed by two individuals at 12.25pm. The cashier on duty was Ms Helen Bedworth. She says that one of the robbers may have been female due to the fact that blond plaits were seen protruding from the hood of the sweatshirt the robber was wearing. While one robber demanded money from the cashier, the other pointed a weapon at the customers present in the foyer of the bank.

4 The passive form of verbs is used because this text is formal.

5 The report is written in full sentences.

3 Work with a partner. You are going to write the next paragraph of the incident report.

1 Read these notes from the police officer's interview with the cashier. Then rewrite them in formal English for the incident report. Remember to:
- use formal vocabulary
- write in full sentences
- use the passive form of verbs where necessary.

> Other people there – old woman, man in suit, possibly another –
> cashier can't remember. Man put bag – black sports bag – on counter.
> Told cashier to fill it.

4 Work with the partner who did the role play on page 56 with you.

1 Refresh your memory by doing the role play between the police officer and the businessman again. Use the questions you wrote down to help you.

2 Now work on your own. Make informal notes from the interview with the businessman. You are going to use them to write the next part of the incident report. Remember to:
- use informal vocabulary   • use abbreviations.

You need not write in full sentences – you can miss out verbs and the word 'the'.

3 Use your notes to write the next part of the formal incident report. You could start:

> Another witness, businessman David Taylor, was in the bank. He states quite
> clearly that ... He also confirms that ... However, he ...

4 Read through the notes and the report you have written. Check that:
- the notes are informal   • the report is formal.

5 Work as a class.

1 With a partner, pick out examples of formal and informal English from each other's notes and report.

2 Share your work with the class.

5.3   Using descriptive detail

This section will help you to:
- write an eye-witness account of a traffic accident
- make good use of description to help the reader understand what happened

1   **Work as a class. You are going to play the descriptions game.**

  1   Choose one person to stand at the front of the class and think of an object. They must describe the object but not say what it is.

  2   The rest of the class must listen carefully and try to guess what is being described. The person who guesses correctly takes the place of the person at the front of the class.

  3   If no one guesses, the object is revealed and the class decides on two details that would have helped them to identify the object.

2   **Work as a class. Read the eyewitness account on a police accident report form below and the notes around it. Then answer these questions.**

  1   Why is the weather an important detail here?

  2   Which are the most important details in this accident report? Explain why.

  3   Can you find any details that are not important to the accident?

1 Details like time, colour, speed and position are as precise as possible.

2 Verbs are descriptive.

> I was walking down Linton High Road last Saturday morning at 9.15. It had been raining and the road was wet. There was a blue mini parked a bit too close to the junction so I couldn't see the corner clearly. Suddenly, a red Ford Focus came around the
> 5   corner doing at least 60 miles an hour. It clipped the front bumper of the mini and went into a spin. It turned twice and ended up across the road blocking it. Almost immediately, a police car sped around the corner also doing about 60 miles an hour. It didn't have time to stop and crashed straight into the red Ford
> 10   Focus. Two men jumped out of the Ford Focus, ran towards the supermarket and disappeared down a side alley, followed by two policemen.

3 **Work in pairs. Read the eyewitness account below, then do this work.**

1 Identify the details that are important to the accident.

2 Identify the details that are not important to the accident.

3 Rewrite the account with only the details important to the accident.

> It was last Friday, the 5th May. I had been to visit my aunt Freda who was having trouble with her feet. She needed some shopping. I was walking down Antwerp Street when I saw this cat run out into the road. It was a lovely cat, a beautiful ginger cat with a long fluffy coat. It ran in front of a Renault Clio, a dark blue one. The driver, a woman about 35, couldn't have stopped in time. She swerved sharply. She must have been frightened. The road was also very wet from the rain. Anyway, she swerved right across the pavement and crashed through the window of the dry cleaner's, the one that always has special offers in the window.

4 **Work with the same partner. You are going to write an eyewitness account.**

1 Examine the picture below. Discuss what has happened.

2 Now work on your own. Write an eyewitness account as if you had been there.

5 **Work with your partner.**

1 First check your own work. Try to correct it. Have you included all the important details? Have you put in any details that are not necessary?

2 Now check each other's work.

5.4 Listening for bias

This section will help you to:
- listen for bias in a famous law case

1 **Work as a class. Read the information below about the case of Craig and Bentley. Then discuss these questions.**

> **1** What could Bentley have meant when he said, 'Let him have it, Chris!'?
>
> *He could have meant … or he might have meant …*
>
> **2** Why do you think they hanged Bentley?
>
> *The jury thought Bentley's words meant …*
>
> **3** Should Bentley have been hanged? Give your reasons.

The case of Craig and Bentley

In November 1952 Christopher Craig (16) and Derek Bentley (19) were seen breaking into a warehouse. The police were called and surrounded the building. They climbed onto the roof to arrest the boys. Bentley surrendered straight away. Craig resisted arrest, and shot and killed a police officer. Bentley was supposed to have said, 'Let him have it, Chris!' before the shot was fired. Bentley said later he didn't know Chris was armed. They were both tried for murder. Hanging was still the punishment for murder in 1952. Craig was too young to be hanged and was given life imprisonment. Bentley was hanged even though:

- Craig, not Bentley, shot and killed the police officer
- Bentley was under arrest at the time Craig fired the gun
- Bentley said at his trial that the police told him what to write in his statement
- Bentley had no record of violent behaviour.

> **Key term**
>
> **bias** – when someone gives a very one-sided view

---

 2 **Work as a class. Read the key term box above, then listen to your teacher read the text opposite and look at the notes. Discuss this question:**

- What did Bentley say during the trial that might mean his statement was not necessarily the truth? Hint – Did Bentley know that Craig had a gun?

1 The judge didn't tell the jury Bentley couldn't read or write.

2 Bentley couldn't read and write, so he couldn't check his statement.

At the end of a trial the judge is expected to sum up the case fairly to help the jury to decide on a verdict. The judge in the Craig and Bentley case said:

'… in his statement he (Bentley) said: "I didn't know he was going to use the gun". Again, if he said that, it shows that he knew it.

Then later in his statement he said he did not know Chris had a gun till he shot. That, of course, is quite **inconsistent** with what he said earlier in his statement.'

inconsistent – when two things can't both be true

3 Listen to your teacher read more of the judge's words below. Discuss these questions with a partner, then as a class.

1 Why do you think the judge mentions common sense?

The judge wants the jury to think …

2 Which line shows the judge's biased view most strongly?

'The first thing that you have to consider is: Did Bentley know that Craig was armed? … The great virtue of trial by jury is that jurymen can exercise the common sense of ordinary people. Can you suppose for a moment, especially when you have heard Craig say that why he carried a revolver was for the purpose of boasting and making himself a big man, that he would not have told his pals he was out with that he had got a revolver? Is it not almost **inconceivable** that Craig would not have told him, and probably shown him the revolver which he had?'

inconceivable – unthinkable

4 Work as a class. Write the ways in which the judge was biased as bullet points.

- *'Common sense', not evidence, will find Bentley …*
- *The judge says that Craig must have told Bentley …*

5 Work as a class. Use the bullet points to write a paragraph to show how the judge was biased.

6 Making information interesting

This unit will help you to:
- put information together
- make information interesting
- learn more about paragraphs

6.1 Getting to the point

This section will help you to:
- find information in a magazine article
- present the information you found in a different way
- make notes

1 Work as a class. You are going to look at how magazines make information interesting.

1 Which magazines do you read? Talk about what you like about them.

2 Information can be boring – try reading a bus timetable! Yet magazines are full of information that the editors present in interesting and entertaining ways. Talk about how the writing in magazines is made entertaining.

> Interesting topics

> Lively pictures

2 Work as a class. Read the magazine article about teenage cancer on the next two pages. Then complete these tasks.

1 This article is basically in two main parts. What are they?

2 Which part is easier to find your way around? Why?

3 The article is designed to help young people become informed about cancer. Note down quickly as many useful things as possible that you can learn from it.

4 Find *three* positive things about cancer – the sorts of things you might put on a poster.

TEENAGE CANCER

Think you've got it tough? Then read about Ruthie, who has battled with cancer ...

What is cancer?

Cancer is a result of cells in your
5 body dividing more quickly than
they should. They cause a lump
(known as a tumour). Which is bad
news. Luckily, catching the cancer
early means that the cells can
10 usually be stopped.

Who does it affect?

The most important thing to
remember is that cancer is a disease
and you can't just catch it like you
15 would a cold. It can be caused by a
variety of things, like too much sun
exposure, the wrong diet or
smoking. Check out what you can
do to reduce your risk now.

◆ Eat smart
20
You may moan when Mum and
Dad nag you to eat your greens,
but they've got a point – almost a
third of all cancer cases are related
25 to what you eat. A healthy
balanced diet is gonna help you,
so only eat fast food as an
absolute treat.

◆ Cover up
30 Get sussed about sun safety. Y'see,
a tan is a sign that your skin's been
damaged by UV rays from the sun.
We do need sunshine for essential
vitamins, but make sure you always
35 slap on plenty of sun cream.

◆ Smoking dangers

Smoking is also responsible for
a cancer-related death every
15 minutes in the UK alone.
40 Our advice – just don't start.

Treatment

You'll probably be one of the lucky
ones, but if it does happen to you,
there's plenty of help out there.
45 **Surgery** If doctors catch the
cancer early enough, a simple
operation to remove the tumour
may be enough to wave goodbye
to it forever.
50 **Radiotherapy** When the tumour
looks like it's confined to one area
of the body, high-energy X-rays
may be used to destroy the cancer
cells. The X-rays are painless,
55 although the skin may feel a bit
sore after the session.
Chemotherapy This uses drugs
which are absorbed into the
bloodstream and can reach cancer
60 cells all over the body.

Don't worry ...

65 It's unlikely that you'll ever get
cancer but it's important to be
clued up about the disease and
know the facts. If you're worried,
talk to an adult you trust. There are
loads of teenagers out there who
prove that cancer can be beaten.

Ruthie's story

'Last year, I got a pain under my arm, which I thought was from messing around in the garden. After a week, I was beginning to
5 feel like I had flu too, so Mum took me to the doctor to get it checked out. At first, he thought it was glandular fever. Eventually I was taken to hospital
10 where I had lots of tests. Six weeks after I visited the doctor, I was diagnosed with a rare form of cancer called ALCL. When they told me, I was so ill I can't really
15 remember how I felt. I think I was relieved they finally knew what was wrong with me.

'I was taken to Manchester Children's Hospital. I did think
20 "Why me?" but seeing all the other young people in the ward were just as unlucky was a bit of a comfort. I had two weeks of intensive chemotherapy and then
25 a week at home. Because my cancer was so rare, I had about six treatments a day whereas the other young people in the ward only had one! The drugs meant I
30 got loads of ulcers in my mouth, so I couldn't eat, but they made me put on weight, too. One of the worst parts of the treatment was losing my hair. Little children
35 would point and stare at me. I did get to go blonde though, as all teenage cancer patients are provided with a wig if they want one, so I chose one with long,
40 blonde hair.

Manchester Children's Hospital

'I wore it when I went back to school after eight months. I was nervous at first but now I'm back, I don't think that I've missed
45 much. I was expecting everyone to ask me loads of questions but no one really said anything. My mum had told them what was wrong with me when I was first
50 diagnosed. I found that loads of my friends avoided talking to me about my experience.

'My cancer is in remission (almost disappeared) now and
55 things are pretty much back to normal. It has changed my life though – I'm not bothered about getting a tan any more and I'd never smoke. They think my
60 cancer was something to do with pollution, so it's made me aware of what we do to our environment. I'd like to be a doctor when I'm older so that I
65 can help others.'

Adapted from *Mizz*, 29 May 2002
© *Mizz* / IPC Syndication

3 **Work in pairs. Look back at the article on pae 65 and note down the information you need to do these tasks.**

> **1** Copy and complete these sentences giving information about cancer treatment.
>
> > **A** S_____ means that _____ .
> >
> > **B** R_____ means that _____ .
> >
> > **C** When someone has ch_____ , _____ .
>
> **2** Now add *three* pieces of advice to complete this paragraph.
>
> > Here are three things you can do to make it less likely that you'll get cancer:
> >
> > - _____
> > - _____
> > - _____
>
> **3** How did you find the information you needed in the text? Discuss and list the features that helped you.

4 **Work on your own. Copy and complete these sentences for a poster to show teenagers that cancer need not be as bad as people fear.**

> **Ruthie's story – not so bad**
>
> It wasn't so bad to be told I had cancer because …
>
> It wasn't so bad to be going into the cancer ward because …
>
> It was pretty bad when my hair fell out but at least …
>
> It wasn't so bad when I went back to school because …
>
> It was pretty bad at the time but now at least …

6.2 **5** **Work as a class.**

> **1** Share your answers about Ruthie's story. Which ones are cleares
>
> **2** You could use the best sentences to produce a poster of Ruthie's

6.2

Different types of writing

This section will help you to:
- recognise different types of writing in a magazine article
- be ready to vary your own writing
- see the differences between paragraphs

1 Work as a class. Think about the magazines and newspapers you read.

> **1** What do you enjoy most in a magazine or newspaper?
>
> **2** What parts of a newspaper or magazine do you find boring?

2 Work as a class. Read the text in the box, then do the work below.

Magazines usually contain:
- material about personal experience or feelings
- information   • advice.

You can write your own material for magazines if you can understand and manage these three kinds of writing.

TEENAGE CANCER

Think you've got it tough? Then read about Ruthie, who has battled with cancer ...

1 Look at these six extracts from the article on teenage cancer. Decide whether each one is about personal experience, information or advice.

> **A** ... cancer is a disease ...
>
> **B** ... I had about six treatments a day ...
>
> **C** ... a tan is a sign that your skin's been damaged ...
>
> **D** ... make sure you always slap on plenty of sun cream ...
>
> **E** ... loads of my friends avoided talking to me about my experience.
>
> **F** ... it's important to be clued up about the disease ...

2 Look again at the magazine article on pages 65 and 66.
   a Does the opening of each paragraph give you an idea of what is coming next? If so, how?

   b Discuss the different ways the paragraphs start.

   Paragraphs about personal experience use 'I' or ...

3 **Work in pairs.**

> **1** Make a copy of the chart below.
>
> | Personal experience | Information | Advice |
> |---|---|---|
> | | | |
>
> **2** Put extracts **A–F** opposite into the correct columns.
>
> **3** Now decide which column each of the following extracts should go into. Add them to your chart.
>
> > **G** I was taken to Manchester Children's Hospital.
> > **H** Get sussed about sun safety.
> > **I** I'm not bothered about getting a tan any more …
> > **J** X-rays are painless …
> > **K** … talk to an adult you trust.
> > **L** … a simple operation to remove the tumour may be enough …

4 **Work on your own. Add these extracts to your chart.**

> > **M** … only eat fast food as an absolute treat.
> > **N** It's unlikely that you'll ever get cancer …
> > **O** I was so ill I can't really remember how I felt.
> > **P** Check out what you can do …
> > **Q** Little children would point and stare at me.
> > **R** … all teenage cancer patients are provided with a wig …

5 **Work as a class. Look at your charts together.**

> **1** Discuss any extracts which you have placed in different columns.
>
> **2** Explain how you made your choices.

6.3

Writing for a magazine

This section will help you to:
- write a non-fiction text about an illness
- make your text interesting

1 Work as a class. In this section you are going to write about an illness or medical condition. Read the box, then do the work below.

> Writing about illness is important. That doesn't mean it has to be boring. The more entertaining it is, the more likely it is that people will read and remember it.

1 Nearly everyone is an expert on some medical matter. Take turns to say a few sentences about an illness or condition you have had. There are some suggestions in the box.

hayfever	glandular fever
SUNSTROKE	food poisoning
migraine	breaking an arm or leg
measles	bronchitis
asthma	chickenpox
burns	allergies

2 Work as a class.

1 Read Ruthie's story on page 66 together. Find the part that deals with each of these topics and see how it is written:
- how the illness started
- how Ruthie felt then
- what the doctors did
- what Ruthie had to go through
- how long the treatment took
- how other people reacted
- how Ruthie is now
- how she feels about her illness now.

2 Take one of the illnesses or medical conditions you talked about earlier. Produce together:
- an opening paragraph about someone's experience
- a piece of information
- a piece of advice.

Ruthie's story

'Last year, I got a pain under my arm, which I thought was from messing around in the garden. After a week, I was beginning to feel like I had flu too, so Mum took me to the doctor to get it checked out. At first, he thought it was glandular fever. Eventually I was taken to hospital where I had lots of tests. Six weeks after I visited the doctor, I was diagnosed with a rare form of cancer called ALCL. When they told me, I was so ill I can't really remember how I felt. I think I was relieved they finally knew what was wrong with me.

'I was taken to Manchester Children's Hospital. I did think "Why me?" but seeing all the other young people in the ward were just as unlucky was a bit of a comfort. I had two weeks of intensive chemotherapy and then a week at home. Because my cancer was so rare, I had about six treatments a day whereas the other young people in the ward only had one! The drugs meant I got loads of ulcers in my mouth, so I couldn't eat, but they made me put on weight, too. One of the worst parts of the treatment was losing my hair. Little children would point and stare at me. I did get to go blonde though, as all teenage cancer patients are provided with a wig if they want one, so I chose one with long, blonde hair.

'I wore it when I went back to school after eight months. I was nervous at first but now I'm back, I don't think that I've missed much. I was expecting everyone to ask me loads of question but no one really said anything. My mum had told them what was wrong with me when I was first diagnosed. I found that loads of my friends avoided talking to me about my experience.

'My cancer is in remission (almost disappeared) now and things are pretty much back to normal. It has changed my life though – I'm not bothered about getting a tan any more and I'd never smoke. They think my cancer was something to do with pollution, so it's made me aware of what we do to our environment. I'd like to be a doctor when I'm older so that I can help others.'

Adapted from Mizz, 29 May 2002
© Mizz / IPC Syndication

3 **Work in pairs.**

1 Tell each other about an illness or medical condition that you know something about. Try to include:
- some personal experience (it doesn't have to be your own)
- some information
- some advice.

> I had asthma first when I was ...
> Most people with asthma use an inhaler ...
> Be careful not to use an inhaler more than ...

2 Write up in rough what you told your partner. This is your *first draft*.

3 Read each other's first drafts. Suggest ways to improve them, for example: *You could say more about ...*

4 **Work on your own. You are going to write the text for your own article for a teenage magazine.**

1 Use your first draft as the start of your article. Add more details about the illness. If you don't have enough to say about one illness, you could write more briefly about two or three. Try to include:
- *one* personal story
- *three* pieces of information
- *three* pieces of advice.

Remember: Your article has got to grab people's attention. Try to remember how the article on pages 65–66 made you want to read it.

5 **Work as a class.**

1 Share *one* piece of information, *one* piece of advice and *one* paragraph from each of your personal stories.

2 You could turn your work into a class medical book. Who could you ask to check that what you have written is accurate?

7 Analysing advice

This unit will help you to:
- offer advice in role play and writing
- understand an author's point of view in advice texts
- look at humour in advice texts

7.1 Giving personal advice

This section will help you to:
- revise the ways you give advice
- develop your role-playing skills
- explore giving advice from different points of view

1 Work as a class. First look at these four different ways of giving advice. Then do the tasks below.

I want to be a pop star but I don't know where to start.

Why don't you join a local band?

You could enter talent shows.

Audition for the school concert!

If I were you, I'd take singing lessons.

1 Which is the best way of offering strong *(authoritative)* advice?

2 Give advice in *four* ways to the Year 9 student with this problem.

I want to learn about computers but I don't know where to start.

2 Work as a class. Look at this problem and at the advice Sophie is given. Read the notes around the advice, then complete the tasks that follow.

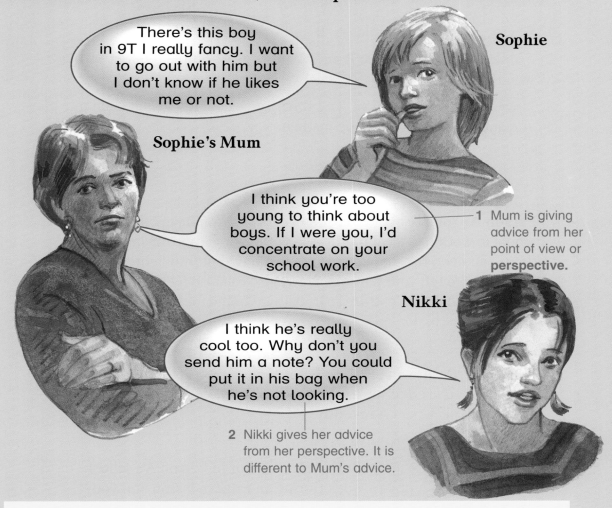

Sophie

There's this boy in 9T I really fancy. I want to go out with him but I don't know if he likes me or not.

Sophie's Mum

I think you're too young to think about boys. If I were you, I'd concentrate on your school work.

1 Mum is giving advice from her point of view or **perspective.**

Nikki

I think he's really cool too. Why don't you send him a note? You could put it in his bag when he's not looking.

2 Nikki gives her advice from her perspective. It is different to Mum's advice.

1 Choose three people to role play Mum and Nikki giving advice to Sophie in front of the class. Discuss the following points before they begin:

- How should Sophie's Mum stand and speak when she is advising Sophie?
- How should Nikki stand and speak?
- How might both conversations continue?

3 Work in pairs. You are going to role play what happens when Sophie asks her form tutor or another adult for advice on her problem.

1 a Discuss what advice the form tutor or other adult might give.

   b Discuss how the form tutor or other adult might stand and speak.

2 Do the role play *twice*. Take it in turns to be Sophie and the person giving advice.

4 **Work in groups of three. You are going to do *two* role plays where people give advice.**

1 Decide who will play roles **A**, **B** and **C**.

2 Think about what advice **B** and **C** might give. Think about how they would stand and speak.

3 Now do the two role plays. The third person should watch each role play and suggest ways it could be made better.

> **Person A:** You are about fourteen years old. You have been missing school to work in a local hairdresser's shop or garage during school time. You need the money because you have got into debt and are frightened to tell your parents. However, you also feel guilty about missing lessons and you are scared about being found out. You want to know what to do.

> **Person B:** You are an old friend of Person A. You are in the same class and you used to see each other out of school, but you haven't seen much of Person A recently.

> **Person C:** You are an adult learning mentor in Person A's school. You see Person A once a week during an English lesson and you have a good relationship with them.

5 **Work as a class. Share some of your role plays.**

1 After each role play, pick out *three* things that were good.

2 Pick out *one* thing that could be improved. Suggest what the group should do to improve it.

7.2 Looking at a writer's viewpoint

This section will help you to:
- read different examples of written advice
- identify a writer's viewpoint in a piece of written advice
- see how the writer's viewpoint affects meaning

 1 Work as a class. Read the pieces of advice about going to college below. Then answer these questions.

1 What does each writer think about going to college?

2 Which of these people might have written each text?
- a school careers advisor
- a college lecturer
- an elderly person who didn't go to college

3 How did you decide who might have written each text?

A

It is really important to earn your own wages as soon as you can. My advice to young people is to get out and get a job. If you want to study, you can go to night school and pay for it yourself. There's no need for the taxpayer to pay for you sitting around on your backside reading books all day.

B

Going to college is a good thing – everyone should go. It gives you time to study something in more depth. It also gives you time to really think what you want to do after you've finished. It means you end up in a job you enjoy.

C

What is important is that you do something for the right reasons. It doesn't matter if that is going to college or getting a job, as long as you have thought about it carefully and it is right for you.

Work as a class. Read the article below and the notes around it, then answer these questions.

1 What is the writer's viewpoint about bringing up girls? Use your own words to explain.

2 Which sentence in the first paragraph gives the writer's viewpoint about bringing up girls?

Advice for parents of daughters

The days are long gone when girls were educated to be good wives and mothers. However, our daughters are still trapped in particular jobs and, more often than not, end up
5   with most of the domestic chores. As parents, we can help break this pattern.

Girls are not often offered the opportunity to help mend broken things around the house. However, given the chance, they often love to
10 do this kind of thing. So when a job arises that would traditionally be offered to a boy, like changing a plug, offer it to your daughter.

When watching the television or a film, teach your daughter *and* your son to question
15 **stereotypes**. These are very powerful and can undo all the good work you have been doing at home.

If your daughter has a problem of some kind, don't be tempted to jump in with a solution.
20 This kind of help actually undermines her confidence. Let her try to sort it out for herself.

1 The writer sets out the problem and tells the reader their viewpoint.

2 In this paragraph the writer gives an example of the problem and some advice on what to do about it.

stereotype – a fixed idea about how a certain type of person should look or behave

3 Work as a pair. Read the whole article opposite again together, then complete these tasks.

1 Look at the third paragraph again. Give an example of a stereotype that you have seen on television.

2 Why does the writer say that sons should question stereotypes too?

3 Find *two* pieces of advice that the writer gives parents of girls.

4 Look at the fourth paragraph again. Why does the writer say that letting a daughter sort out a problem for herself would be better?

 4 Work on your own. Write about the the advice in the article you have just read. Use these sentence starters to help you.

The writer of this article thinks ...

This idea is introduced in ...

The rest of the article ...

One piece of advice given is ...

I think *(give your own opinion here)* ...

5 Work as a class. Share what you have written about the article.

1 Check that what you have written about the article is correct.

2 Discuss as a class your opinions about what the author says in the article. Explain why you agree or disagree.

Writing impersonal advice

This section will help you to:
- write impersonal advice
- write advice which expresses no opinion

1 **Work as a class. Talk about what is different about these types of advice.**

> **A** The advice you give to your friend who has fallen out with their dad.
>
> **B** Advice to students about choosing their options.

7.6 **2** **Work as a class. Read the advice for parents below together. Look at the notes around the text and complete these tasks.**

> **1** Why has the writer put their profession next to their name?
>
> **2** Make a list of other topics that might be included in this article.

Advice for parents: How to help your son or daughter revise

Written by J. Lynch, Headteacher, Danford Secondary School

It's a worrying time for parents when their sons and daughters are sitting exams. It's
5 also difficult to know how to help. Follow the advice below and the student in your family will cope with everything the exam season brings.

Make sure the student has a quiet place to
10 study with a clear, uncluttered desk. They may want to listen to music while they study. This is fine as the music cuts out other background noise.

1 The advice is impersonal because it is a problem lots of students have.

2 The advice sounds authoritative because the writer says it will work.

3 The imperative as strong advice is used here.

4 The impersonal advice in this paragraph talks to no one in particular but to parents generally.

3 Work as a class. You are going to write the next paragraph of the article for parents. It will tell parents how to help with revision planning. Follow these steps.

> 1 Discuss together what you might write about how to plan revision for exams.
>
> > - ***work out how many days …***
> > - ***see how many topics …***
>
> 2 Write the paragraph together. Write *three* sentences. Use an imperative to show strong advice in one of your sentences.

 4 Work on your own. You are going to write the next paragraph of advice to parents. It will be about how to look after a student while they revise.

> 1 Take each of these points and use it in your paragraph.
>
> > Make sure they:
> > - take regular breaks
> > - drink plenty and eat a healthy diet
> > - don't revise for too long at a time.
>
> 2 When you have finished, check your paragraphs against the text opposite. Do they sound similar? Discuss your paragraph with a partner. Ask these questions:
>
> - Does it make sense?
> - Is there an imperative as advice included?
> - Does it talk to parents in general to sound impersonal?

5 Work as a class. Share your articles. Talk about whether they sound the same as the model text.

7.4 Exploring humour in advice texts

> **This section will help you to:**
> - explore humorous advice texts
> - write some humorous advice

1 Work as a class. Look at the book covers on this page and answer these questions.

> **1** Which book offers serious advice and which offers humorous advice?
>
> **2** How did you decide?
>
> **3** What is each book about?

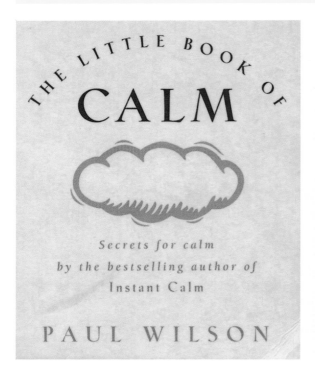

2 Work as a class. Read the key term box. Then look at the texts opposite and the notes around them. Answer this question:

> **Why is the parody funny?**

> **Key term**
>
> **parody** – an imitation that makes fun of a book, a play or a media product

Calm Down Your Diet

1 This is sensible advice if you want to stay calm.

If you want to feel calm, eat more raw fruit and vegetables, yoghurt, milk, eggs, wholegrains, beans, **pulses**, nuts and seeds.

2 The clouds are meant to emphasise the idea of calm.

pulses – beans and lentils

Become a Junk Hunk

Junk food will help you lead a rubbish life.

Eat it as often as you can.

1 This is a **parody** of the original above. It gives advice, but the advice is ridiculous!

2 The lightning is a parody of the original page design, which has calming clouds.

3 Work with a partner. Decide which *two* pieces of advice are serious and which *two* are parody.

> **A** Use a soft voice. Have you ever noticed a calm person with a loud voice?
>
> **B** Go to the cinema. Sit near other people. Hold a conversation with a friend.
>
> **C** Whenever you get the chance, shake up cans and bottles of fizzy drinks. Then leave them for someone else to open.
>
> **D** Offer a compliment. You'll find the good feelings that flow from it will be as much yours as the recipient's.

 4 Work with a partner. Write *two* pieces of humorous advice about creating as much stress as possible in school.

5 Work as a class. Share your advice. Who has written the funniest advice?

8 Arguing your case

This unit will help you to:
- consider how well you speak in different situations
- consider how well you listen in different situations
- argue against someone's point of view
- shape your ideas into a series of linked paragraphs

8.1 Improving how you speak and listen

This section will help you to:
- talk about how well you speak and listen in different situations
- improve the way you work in a group
- discuss the strengths and weaknesses of an argument

 1 **Work as a class.**

1 Brainstorm checklists of things you should remember to do when you are:

- speaking in a class discussion: *raise your hand …*

- talking in a group: *make sure everyone speaks …*

- talking in pairs: *keep to the subject …*

- listening to other people: *wait until other people have finished before …*

2 You have just taken part in a class discussion. Look at your checklist for a class discussion. Write down *one* thing that you need to improve.

 2 **Work as a class. First read the key term box. Then do the work below to find out how to spot the weaknesses in an argument and put forward counter-arguments.**

Key term

counter-argument – the point you make against a weakness in someone's argument

1 Read the first paragraph of the argument opposite. Study the two steps you can use to find the weaknesses in the argument and work out counter-arguments. Look at how to use a chart to note down your ideas.

No more mobiles!

I want to ban students from having mobile phones in school. **They are a complete nuisance** and **our school would be a much happier and calmer place without them**.

5 Teachers would prefer mobiles to be banned because they all spend so much time dealing with lost or stolen phones. Similarly, teachers are annoyed when phones 'accidentally' ring during lessons and assemblies.

There's no reason for students to have mobile phones in school. In fact, it would be better for students if they were
10 banned. After all, students can't receive bullying text messages in school if they don't have phones. In the same way, they might have more friends if they talked to each other rather than gossiping into their phones.

I'm sure parents would like mobiles to be banned in school as
15 well. Not only would they save money on calls, but also they wouldn't worry about their children being mugged for their phones. Moreover, if students don't see each other phoning they won't feel such pressure to have the latest phone.

In fact I can't see any reason not to ban mobile phones
20 straight away. Can you?

Finding the weaknesses in an argument

Step 1 Find a point the writer makes.

- *They are a complete nuisance.*

Check if it is a weakness by asking: *Do I agree with this point?*

- *I don't agree that mobile phones are a complete nuisance.*

Step 2 Decide what the counter-argument is by asking: *Why is my opinion different about this?*

- *Students find them useful to keep in touch with their parents.*

Weaknesses in the headteacher's argument	Your counter-arguments
1 Mobile phones are a complete nuisance 2 No phones – would make school happy and calm	Phones – useful – can call parents Mobiles keep students happy and calm – can arrange to travel home with friends.

2 Now look at the second paragraph. Find the weaknesses in the argument and give a counter-argument for each one. Note your answers in a chart like this.

Weaknesses in the headteacher's argument	Your counter-arguments
3 All teachers ... 4 Teachers annoyed – phones ...	

8.3 3 **Work in a group of three or four. You are going to look at the third paragraph on page 83.**

1 Note the weaknesses and your counter-arguments in your own chart like the one below.

Weaknesses in the headteacher's argument	Your counter-arguments
5 Don't have to worry about ... 6	Can still be ...

2 You have just taken part in a group discussion. Look at your checklist for talking in a group. Write down *one* way that you can still improve.

8.3 4 **Work in pairs. You are going to look at the fourth paragraph on page 83.**

1 Discuss the weaknesses of the headteacher's arguments and your counter-arguments. Note down your ideas on your charts.

2 You have just been talking in a pair. Look back at your checklist. Find *one* thing you did really well.

5 **Work as a class.**

1 Talk about the weaknesses in the headteacher's argument and about your counter-arguments.

2 How did you go about spotting weaknesses in an argument and suggesting counter-arguments?

First we searched for ...
Then we asked ...

3 Does the headteacher's argument have any strengths (points that you agree with)?

8.2 Arguing against someone's point of view

This section will help you to:
- write pairs of paragraphs
- use connectives to link your points and paragraphs
- argue against someone else's point of view

1   **Work as a class. Look at what Sam is saying, then do the tasks below.**

1 You are about to say something that agrees with what Sam has said. Choose *four* connectives from the box below that you could use, for example: *Mobile phones **also** ...*

2 Now you want to say something that disagrees with what Sam has said. Choose *three* suitable connectives from the box, for example: ***However,** mobile phones ...*

3 Find *eight* connectives in the box that need commas when you use them at the start of a sentence.

however	similarly	whereas	despite this	also
on the other hand	but	rather	and though	
nevertheless	moreover	in the same way	because	

4 Now create a counter-argument to what Sam is saying. Remember to use a connective.

Sam says that ...

2 Work as a class. Read the steps below to see how to put your counter-arguments together to give your opposing point of view. Then read the beginning of a student's text opposite and look at the labels around it.

Step 1 Write a short introduction saying what the headmaster's argument is about:

The headteacher argues that our school would be a better place if mobile phones were banned. However, there are several weaknesses in his argument.

Step 2 Decide which weaknesses in your chart are about the same subject. You could use highlighter pen to mark them. Write a topic sentence that tells readers what the group of weaknesses is about:

The headteacher says that the school would be a calmer place without mobiles.

Points 1 and 2 in my chart are both about why the headteacher thinks the school would be calmer without mobiles. I can use them to write two paragraphs that follow on from each other.

Step 3 Now you are going to write a paragraph about the first weakness. First say what point the headteacher made:

The headteacher argues that mobile phones are a complete nuisance.

Step 4 Introduce your counter-argument with a connective that shows you disagree with the headteacher's point:

However, phones can be useful …

Step 5 Now write your next linked paragraph.

- Begin the paragraph with a connective that shows it has something in common with the last paragraph: *Similarly the headteacher …*
- Repeat steps 3 and 4 for the next weakness you have found.

Step 6 Now repeat steps 2 to 5 for the next group of weaknesses you have found.

Weaknesses in the headteacher's argument	Your counter-arguments
1 Mobile phones are a complete nuisance	Phones – useful – can call parents
2 No phones – would make school happy and calm	Mobiles keep students happy and calm – can arrange to travel home with friends

Why mobile phones should not be banned in school

The headteacher argues that our school would be a better place if mobile phones were banned. However, there are several weaknesses in his argument.

1 Write a short introduction (Step 1).

The headteacher says that the school would be a calmer place without mobiles. He argues that mobile phones are a complete nuisance. **However,** mobile phones are useful because students who are going to be home late can phone their parents to stop them worrying.

2 This sentence says what this group of weaknesses are about (Step 2).

3 This is the first point the headteacher made (Step 3).

4 Use a connective to show you disagree: *However, ...* (Step 4).

Similarly the headteacher argued that schools would be calmer and happier places without mobile phones. **However,** students feel calm and happy at school if they can use a mobile phone to arrange to go home with friends.

Work in a group of three or four. You are going to use the chart below to write the next *two* paragraphs of your opposing point of view.

1 Step 2: Start with a topic sentence summing up what this group of weaknesses is about:

The headteacher argues …

2 Complete the first paragraph using weakness 3 and your counter-argument.

  a Step 3: Write a sentence pointing out what the first weakness is:

   He says that …

  b Step 4: Use a connective from your list to show that the next point disagrees with the last one:

   _____, *this problem could be overcome by …*

3 Step 5: Now write your second linked paragraph using weakness 4 and your counter-argument. Choose a different connective from the list you made on page 85 to show that it has something in common with the last one:

   _____, *the headteacher argues that …*

Weaknesses in the headteacher's argument	Your counter-arguments
3 All teachers waste time dealing with stolen or lost phones	Could have just one teacher or person in charge of dealing with lost or stolen phones
4 Teachers annoyed – phones 'accidentally' ring in lessons and assemblies	Remind students to turn phones off before lesson or assembly starts

4 Work on your own. Write the next two linked paragraphs. Use the chart and sentence starters below to help you. Follow Steps 2 to 6 from page 86.

The headteacher thinks that banning mobile phones will improve students' … .
He says that … ….., people can be bullied … It is better to tell students to …

…, he says that … . ….. students are able to …

Weaknesses in the headteacher's argument	Your counter-arguments
5 Don't have to worry about nasty text messages from bullies if don't have mobile in school	Can still be bullied on phone at home
6 Students would have more friends if they didn't waste time gossiping into their mobiles	Mobiles help students keep in touch with their friends – make friendships stronger

Connectives to use:
- **when you disagree:** however, but, on the other hand, rather
- **when you agree:** similarly, in the same way

 5 Work as a class.

1 First work in pairs. Check each other's pair of paragraphs.
   - Underline each sentence that explains a weakness in the headteacher's argument.
   - Circle the connectives used to show the writer disagrees with the headteacher's view.
   - Put a star by the connective which introduces the second paragraph.

2 Work as a class. Talk about how you went about turning your notes into pairs of paragraphs.

3 Work together to write a concluding paragraph for your opposing point of view. Look back to page 83 to see how the headteacher concluded his argument. Start like this:

In my opinion, …

suading ders

9.1 Understanding how advertisements are written

This section will help you to:
- find out how advertisements persuade readers
- work out how an advertisement suits its readers

1 Work as a class. Brainstorm a list of four different adverts you have seen on television that sell something (a product). For each one decide:

- what it is selling (the product)
- how the advert makes the product seem attractive

  > It makes the product sound ...

- who the advert is aimed at (the audience)

  > Young adults who ...

2 Work as a class. First read the key terms box, then read the advertisement on pages 92 and 93. Read the labels to find out how every sentence in an advert is used to persuade the audience. Then answer these questions.

Key terms

alliteration – when the sound a word begins with is repeated at the start of another word nearby, for example: *pick your picture.*

onomatopoeia – when the sound of a word suggests its meaning, for example: *hiss, bang.*

1 What is the advert selling (the product)?

2 What sort of people would this advert appeal to (the target audience)?

3 How does the writer make sure the audience will want to buy the phone?

4 How has the writer used slang, alliteration and onomatopoeia to make the advert more exciting? Find *one* example of each not given in the labels.

3 Work in pairs. Read the advertisement on page 94. Decide which sentence does each of these jobs.

> **A** Tells readers the facts about what the gum can do.
>
> **B** Instructs readers to use the gum.
>
> **C** Warns readers.
>
> **D** Makes a joke – uses a pun on the name of the product.
>
> **E** Suggests to readers that people will be dazzled by their teeth if they use this gum.

4 Work in pairs.

> **1** What audience might the advertisement for Orbit Ice White appeal to?
>
> > *People who ...*
>
> **2** What has the writer said and done to make the target audience want to buy this gum? Use these sentence starters to help you.
>
> > *First the writer helps the reader to imagine ...*
> >
> > *Next the reader is told ...*
> >
> > *Then the writer says ...*
> >
> > *Finally the reader is instructed ... A pun is used ...*

5 Work as a class. List the different ways a writer can use sentences to persuade a reader to buy something.

> > • *A writer can write a sentence that boasts or ...*
> > • *A writer can use all ...*

Fotofone – the best in shoot and send

What a fan-tastic shot!

1 The writer uses two puns – the *shot* (picture) on the phone shows a *fan*.

When your team's a winner, you want the world to know! It's so easy to show your mates at home with **Fotofone**.
5 Just pick your picture, point and press. Your photos will amaze your friends. And that's not all! **Fotofone** has wacky ring tones and great games, and it gives
10 you all the best info. Zoom to your nearest High Street to find **Fotofone** – it's a fan-tastic bargain!

2 This sentence tells you a **reason** why the phone's special feature is a good idea.

3 This sentence **describes** using the phone. It makes it sound fun and easy to use. There are lots of words starting with the same sound (**alliteration**). This helps make the sentence sound snappy.

4 This sentence tells you more **facts** about what the phone can do. It uses **slang** words (*wacky*) and **onomatopoeia** (*ring*) to make it more appealing to the target audience.

5 This last sentence is an **instruction**. It tells you where to buy the phone. It repeats the word *fan-tastic*.

games

choose from four cool colours

24 ring tones

Mobile

information

Fotofone

Caution: Never stare directly at Orbit Ice White teeth.

Orbit Ice White helps reduce tooth stains that can build up
throughout the day, helping to keep your teeth naturally clean and white.
So much so, other people may need some protection.

Help knock tooth stains into orbit.

9.2 Writing a question and answer slogan

This section will help you to:
- understand how writers use word play in slogans
- write a question and answer slogan
- use a thesaurus

1 Work as a class. You are going to see how writers choose the best words for their adverts.

> **1** There are often several words that express the same idea, but one of them will sound the best in your sentence. Use a thesaurus to make a list of words that you can use instead of 'new'.
>
> > **Key term**
> >
> > **slogan** – a short and catchy saying which makes sure the audience remembers the name of the product and something special about it. The slogan is often used at the end of an advert, for example: *Help knock tooth stains into orbit.*
>
> **2** Read the key term box above. Then list as many slogans from different advertisements as you can in two minutes.
>
> > *Mr Muscle — loves the jobs you hate.*
> > *Nescafé — The Coffee Lover's Coffee*
> > *Maybe she's born with it. Maybe it's Maybelline.*
>
> **3** Look at each of your slogans and talk about why it was easy to remember. It may be for one of the three reasons below.
>
> > **A** Words in the slogan are linked by repeated words or sounds, for example:
> > *Nescafé – The Coffee Lover's Coffee*
> > *My Style. My City. My Scene.*
> > *Mars – Pleasure you can't measure.*
> >
> > **B** Words in the slogan are linked by a play on words, for example:
> > *Don't accept less than MORE TH>N*
> > *HSBC The world's local bank*
> >
> > **C** The slogan is a question and answer, for example:
> > *Who cares what you eat? Birds Eye cares.*

2 Work as a class. You are going to write a question and answer slogan.

> **1** First read the example below to discover one way of writing a question and answer slogan that is easy to remember.
>
> **2** Now follow the three steps to complete this question and answer slogan to make young women want to buy a mobile phone called Gold:
>
> *Want …? …Gold.*

Writing a question and answer slogan

Step 1 If the product's name is a real word, brainstorm words to do with that name. Use a thesaurus to help you, but think of your own words as well.

The product is a mobile phone called Diamond.

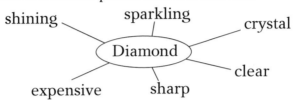

Step 2 Brainstorm words that describe what the product does for the audience.

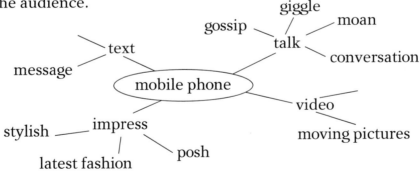

Step 3 Use ideas from your brainstorming to help you write a question and answer slogan. Try out different words until you decide you have found the best slogan for your audience:

Want ~~shiny~~ crystal clear pictures? Get a Diamond

    1 'crystal clear' is better than 'shiny' – but perhaps this audience is more interested in talk than pictures.

Want sparkling conversation? Get a Diamond.

    2 This is better because it suggests a Diamond phone can even make their conversations more interesting.

9.2 3 Work in pairs. Follow the three steps on page 96 to complete these slogans for mobile phones.

> **A** Want _____ ? _____ Chatterphone
> (Audience: girls aged about 19)
>
> **B** Want _____ ? _____ Winner
> (Audience: sports fans)

4 Work on your own. Work out your best question and answer slogan for a mobile phone called Star aimed at 18-year-old boys.

> Want _____ ? _____ Star

5 Work as a class. Share your best slogans.

> **1** Talk about what makes each slogan easy to remember. Is there any way you can improve it?
>
> **2** Talk about how you worked out a question and answer slogan.
>
> **3** Your slogans for Chatterphone and Star are for an audience in their late teens. Decide which slogan works best for this audience. Can you think of a better one now?

9.3 Comparing different ways of organising paragraphs

This section will help you to:
- try out different ways of organising a paragraph
- decide how to make the paragraph really persuasive

1 Work as a class.

1 Brainstorm what you know about writing in paragraphs.

The first sentence says ...

2 Look back at the work you did in the last section. What jobs might different sentences do in an advertisement?

- *Instruct the audience ...*
- *Describe ...*
- *Give facts ...*

2 Work as a class. The paragraph on the opposite page is taken from an advertisement. Read the text and the labels around it to find out why the paragraph was organised in this way.

3 Work in a group. Read the sentences below. You are going to use them in an advert selling a mobile phone called Matchfone to football fans. Decide which is the best order to put them in to make the paragraph really persuasive.

A Know the score. Get a Matchfone.	(Instruction)
B With texting, over 50 different ring tones and 30 games to play, this phone will make sure you're a winner.	(Facts)
C With a Matchfone you'll be a key player. With this phone in your pocket you'll be ahead of the crowd and in on all the best moments.	(Reasons)
D Don't be caught offside.	(Warning)

1 I want to grab my audience's attention straight away. They are business people. I tell them the most important thing that this phone can do for them first.

2 Next I give the audience reasons to want to buy this mobile phone rather than any other.

Have all the facts and figures at your fingertips!

With its **unique** notepad and diary feature you will always be ready for that important call or vital meeting. And since a PA phone has e-mail
5 functions and Internet access you can keep in touch with all your clients, no matter where you are or what they're doing. Amazingly, a PA phone gives you space for 1000 entries in its address book
10 and has a large display screen to make your diary, web pages and e-mails easy to read. Our stylish e-pen makes the keypad incredibly easy to use and you can even scribble handwritten notes on
15 your diary pages.

Go on. Keep a personal assistant in your pocket. Get a PA.

3 Then I tell the audience some impressive facts about the mobile phone

4 I finish the advert with a memorable slogan that instructs the audience to go out and get one of these mobile phones.

unique – the only one of its type
PA – short for 'personal assistant'

4 Work in pairs. Write a paragraph advertising a mobile phone called Freedom to mothers. Decide the best order for these seven sentences to go in.

> **A** Freedom's Internet access makes the weekly grind of supermarket shopping a thing of the past.
>
> **B** And this phone's diary feature lets you make appointments and organise the school run at the touch of a button.
>
> **C** With a Freedom phone you'll have more time for yourself.
>
> **D** You'll have more time to chat to friends, too, and to arrange treats and surprises.
>
> **E** Go on Mum, you deserve it. Enjoy your Freedom!
>
> **F** Make time for yourself.
>
> **G** Text messaging saves you and the family hassle – no more worrying about where they are.

5 Work as a class. Share your finished paragraphs. Explain why you put the sentences in the order you chose.

9.4 Using facts and reasons to persuade an audience

This section will help you to:
- write complex sentences
- write persuasively for a particular audience

1 Work as a class. You are going to write an advertisement for a mobile phone that will target young adults.

1 Make a list of at least *six* features the ideal mobile phone for a young adult would have. (These will be the *facts* in your advertisement.)

- *Video messaging*

2 Why is each feature a good idea? (These will be the *reasons* in your advertisement.)

- *Video messaging — young adults like to show their friends what they are doing*

Key term

clause – a group of words containing a verb.
- Every sentence contains at least one **main clause**. A main clause makes sense on its own.
- A complex sentence contains at least one **subordinate clause**. A subordinate clause needs to be joined to a main clause to make a sentence. It does not make sense on its own.

I like my Diamond mobile phone because it can send pictures.

Main clause – makes sense on its own

Subordinate clause – does not make sense on its own.

3 Read the key term box above. Then find a main clause and a subordinate clause in each of these complex sentences.

> **A** Mitch bought a new phone because his old one was broken.
>
> **B** Although it wasn't very expensive, it had lots of good features.
>
> **C** Seeing Mitch's new mobile, Kev was green with envy.

4 Read the explanation box opposite to find out how clauses are used in different types of sentences. Then read the paragraph opposite from the advertisement on pages 92 and 93. Find:
- a simple sentence
- a compound sentence
- a complex sentence.

5 Talk about the effect of using the three different sentence types in this advert.

The simple sentence ... short and catchy.

Explanation

Types of sentences

Sentences are made up of clauses. There are three main types of sentences.

- A **simple sentence** contains one main clause, for example: *I bought a printer.*

- A **compound sentence** contains two or more main clauses joined by the connectives *and*, *or* or *but*.

  The two clauses are equally important, for example: *I bought a printer and Jake bought a scanner.*

- A **complex sentence** has a main clause and one or more subordinate clauses. The clauses can be linked by a connective such as *after, because, who, although* or *when*, for example: *I was broke after I bought my printer.*

  If the subordinate clause comes before the main clause, it is usually followed by a comma: *When I bought my printer, I went into town with Jake.*

  Some complex sentences do not need a connective, for example: *Carrying our heavy bags, Jake and I caught a bus home.*

When your team's a winner, you want the world to know! It's so easy to show your mates at home with **Fotofone**.
5 Just pick your picture, point and press. Your photos will amaze your friends. And that's not all! **Fotofone** has wacky ring tones and great games, and it gives
10 you all the best info. Zoom to your nearest High Street to find **Fotofone** – it's a fan-tastic bargain!

2 Work as a class. First read the box below. It shows you how to write
a persuasive complex sentence that contains a fact and a reason.
Then do this task.

1 You have been asked to write an advertisement for a mobile phone
designed for young adults. It has 52 ring tones. Follow the method in the
box to draft a persuasive complex sentence. Your reason could be: *You can
choose a new ring tone every week of the year.*

Writing a persuasive complex sentence for an advertisement

1 Choose one of the product's features.
The phone has 100 games to choose from.

2 Think of a reason why the feature is a good one.
You'll never get bored.

3 Make your complex sentence persuasive by
starting with the positive information.

- Start your sentence with a subordinate clause
about your product's feature.
- Introduce your clause with a connective from
the box.
- Remember that you may need to finish
your clause with a comma.

because
after
if
until
as
when
since

Because *you can choose from 100 games,*

4 Complete your complex sentence with a main clause giving your
reason. This part of the sentence should make sense on its own.

Because *you can choose from 100 games, you'll never get bored.*

3 **Work in pairs. Write** *four* **persuasive complex sentences telling business people why each feature of this mobile phone is a good idea. Use the method in the box opposite.**

Feature of mobile phone	Reason it's a good idea for a business person
Address book can hold 1000 telephone numbers.	You can keep in touch with all your customers by mobile.
Secrecy button	You can have a private conversation without your caller hearing you.
Security lock	No one can steal your phone or customers' details.
Diary	You don't have to carry a book with you.

4 **Work on your own. Look back at the list of features for a mobile phone for young adults that you made on page 101. Choose** *four* **features to use in complex persuasive sentences. Write your sentences following the method in the box opposite.**

  5 **Work as a class.**

> **1** First work with a partner. Look at each other's sentences. For each sentence ask:
> - Does it make sense?
> - Could it be made more persuasive?
>
> **2** Now work as a class. Talk about how writing complex sentences helped make your writing persuasive.
>
> **3** Work together to write an advertisement for a mobile phone that will appeal to young adults. Choose the most persuasive sentences from activity **4** and use your best slogan from page 97.

10 Understanding the influence of media texts

This unit will help you to:
- find out how reliable a website is
- write about how the same idea is presented in different media
- design a website

10.1 Looking at websites

This section will help you to:
- understand how websites are organised
- look at how a website can be used by the reader

1 **Work as a class. You are going to look at the features of a web page.**

1 Describe the web page opposite.

> The title is ...   The picture shows ...

2 The list below shows features found on many websites. How many of these features can you find on the Christian Aid Global Gang web page opposite?

- Titles
- Photos or graphics
- Links to other parts of the website
- An invitation to the readers to send in their views
- Message board
- Text
- Search facility
- Links to other websites

3 Talk about how the reader can use each feature on the page.

> The title tells you ...

> The reader can use the search facility to ...

4 What audience is the website aimed at?

5 What is the purpose of the website?

1 The page is drawn like a cartoon. Simon Thomas is inserted to look as if he's with the Global Gang.

2 The reader can choose many different ways to interact with the web page.

3 The reader can click here to find out what this charity does.

6 The reader can click on the continents on the globes to find out about children in different parts of the world.

5 The reader can click on each character as another way to go to the pages listed across the bottom.

4 The reader can use different pages of the site for different purposes.

2 **Work as a class. Look back at the Global Gang web page.**

1 How have the designers of the website tried to appeal to their target audience?

2 Talk about whether the layout works well. Give your reasons.

3 Suggest why the links to other pages are repeated around the page.

4 Find *three* different ways the reader can use the features on this web page.

3 **Work with a partner. Look at the Global Gang web page again and answer these questions.**

1 Your friend Carl wants to find out more about Christian Aid. Which bit of the web page should he click on?

2 If Carl clicked on each of the other links, what do you think he would find?

3 Which bits of the web page would you find interesting?

4 How does the layout help you find the links you are interested in?

10.1 4 **Work on your own. Write a paragraph about the web page. Use the sentence starters to help you. Add other comments if you wish.**

> The Global Gang web page is aimed at …
> I know this because …
> The purpose of the web page is …
> The layout of the web page is …
> The features used on this web page are …
> Someone interested in finding out about the charity could look at …
> I would look at …

5 **Work as a class. Share your paragraphs about the Global Gang web page. What are the important things to remember when designing a web page for this audience?**

10.2

Designing a web page

This section will help you to:
- look at how well ways of presenting information on a web page work
- choose ways to present information on a web page
- design part of a web page

1 Work as a class. You are going to talk about what makes a text or web page attractive to children aged about ten.

    1 Brainstorm a list of features that might make ten-year-olds want to look at a book, magazine or web page.

        • ***Bright colours***

    2 Now look again at the Christian Aid Global Gang web page on page 107. Pick out what will definitely appeal to these children. Talk about what the web page tells you (the *content*) and how it looks (the *design*).

    3 How has the designer made the page fun to use?

2 Work as a class.

    1 First read the box below.

> **What you have to do**
>
> Imagine that Christian Aid wants to make the Global Gang home page even more attractive to older children (aged about ten). They are holding a competition for the best web page design. You have to:
> - use the same words as the original web page.
> - use all you know about what appeals to older children
> - use the features that make the web page fun to use.

    2 Chloe has started to design a new Global Gang web page. You can see what she has done so far on the next page. Discuss whether this part of her design is successful.

    3 Brainstorm ideas for completing her web page design.

A photo of ...   She could animate ...

Chloe James
Web page design for Global Gang

Home page

More information

Find out about children from around the world

BACK

GLOBAL GANG

Brightly coloured letters
to make it look fun.

3 Work with a partner. Discuss different ideas of your own for redesigning the Global Gang web page.

10.2 4 Work on your own.

1 Redesign the Global Gang page using the ideas you discussed with your partner above. You might want to start from Chloe's design.

2 Look at the note Chloe made about her design. Make notes around your own web page to explain why you think your design will appeal to older children.

10.3 5 Work as a class. Take it in turns to share your design with the rest of the class. Use your notes to help you explain your design to the class.

10.3

Evaluating the usefulness of a website

This section will help you to:
- look at a website to see if it is useful
- make judgements about how biased a website is

 1   **Work as a class.**

1   First work on your own. Look up each of these words in a dictionary.

> relevance   validity   bias

2   Now work as a class to answer these questions.

    a How would you use each of these words to talk about a website?

> The validity of a website means how up-to-date it is.

    b Why are these ideas important when you are researching a project?

> You need to know about the bias of a website because …

3   On your own, write a definition of each of these *three* words. Your definition should show how the word can be used to talk about a website. Use the example below to help you.

> *Relevance* – The relevance of a website means how useful it is to what I am doing. For example, if I am doing a project on Shakespeare's work, I need websites about the plays and poems of William Shakespeare. Websites about Stratford-on-Avon, where he was born, may be linked, but they may not be relevant to what I am doing. I have to look carefully at my question to decide.

Work as a class. You are going to see how a web page is relevant to a project.

1 Class 9B have been asked to do the following task:

> Write a short persuasive article for the school newspaper called:
> Make smacking children illegal!

Look at the web page below. Then answer these questions.

a What group of people is the web page aimed at (its *target audience*)?

b What is the *purpose* of the web page?

c Look at the date the page was last updated. Is the content still valid?

d Would the page be useful in any way to help Class 9B write the article (is it *relevant*)?

IW
p.187

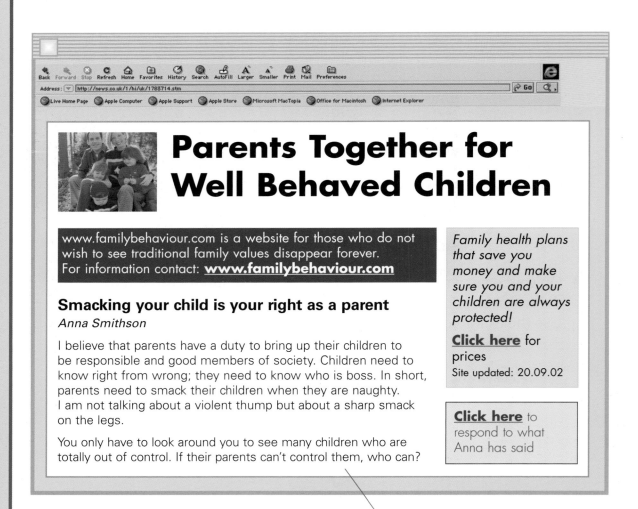

Parents Together for Well Behaved Children

www.familybehaviour.com is a website for those who do not wish to see traditional family values disappear forever.
For information contact: **www.familybehaviour.com**

Family health plans that save you money and make sure you and your children are always protected!

Click here for prices
Site updated: 20.09.02

Click here to respond to what Anna has said

Smacking your child is your right as a parent
Anna Smithson

I believe that parents have a duty to bring up their children to be responsible and good members of society. Children need to know right from wrong; they need to know who is boss. In short, parents need to smack their children when they are naughty. I am not talking about a violent thump but about a sharp smack on the legs.

You only have to look around you to see many children who are totally out of control. If their parents can't control them, who can?

1 The web page is **relevant** to the task because it is about smacking children, but it presents the opposite view.

3 **Work in pairs. Discuss the questions below.**

> **1** Is the content of <u>familybehaviour.com</u> biased? Explain your answer.
>
> **2** What other kinds of websites would the students in 9B need to look at to complete their research for the article?

4 **Work with your partner. First look at the extract from a website below, then answer the questions below. Make sure you can give reasons for your answers.**

> **1** What is the target audience for the website?
>
> **2** What is the purpose of the website?
>
> **3** Is the information on the site valid?
>
> **4** Is the site biased in any way?
>
> **5** Is the site relevant to Class 9B's task?

Stop Cruelty to Children

Hitting children is wrong!

Hitting a child is never right. Children learn nothing from being hit except that violence is all right. Children who have been hit do not learn about other ways of resolving conflicts. It is no wonder that we have so many problems with our young people when we continue to maintain that it is a parent's right to punish their child using physical violence.

Site updated: January 2001

5 **Work as a class. Complete the tasks below.**

> **1** Discuss your answers to the questions in activity **4** above.
>
> **2** How could the five questions you answered be useful when you use the Internet?

10.4

Same idea, different media

Key term

junk mail – anything that arrives through the post which has not been asked for. Junk mail includes adverts, charity leaflets and take-away menus.

 1 Work as a class. First read the key term box above. Next discuss an appropriate ending for each of the sentences below.

> **A charity junk mail leaflet**
>
> **A** The purpose of a charity junk mail leaflet is ＿＿＿＿＿＿ .
>
> **B** A junk mail leaflet has to catch the eye because ＿＿＿＿＿＿ .
>
> **A charity web page**
>
> **C** The purpose of a charity web page is ＿＿＿＿＿＿ .
>
> **D** A charity web page is for people ＿＿＿＿＿＿ .
>
> **E** People who use this web page are likely to want ＿＿＿＿＿＿ .

2 Work as a class. Read the leaflet and the web page on the next two pages and look at the notes around them. Complete the tasks below.

> 1 What is the purpose of the Save the Children leaflet opposite?
>
> 2 What is the purpose of the 'Beat Poverty' web page on page 116?
>
> 3 Find ways in which the leaflet and the web page are designed to suit their audiences.

This is a leaflet published by Save the Children and sent to people through their letterboxes.

1 Sad-looking child looking directly at reader makes the reader feel sympathetic.

2 The heading tells the reader just how little money would make a difference to this girl.

3 Emotive words like 'harsh' persuade the reader of the need to give money.

 10p a day can save her from poverty

There are more child workers in India than any other country worldwide. **Desperate poverty makes working conditions for a child like Rekha harsh and the hours exhaustingly long.** She is paid a pittance to coat glass bangles with gold lacquer – a job that exposes her to toxic materials day after day.

Save the Children's long term aim is to help families escape the poverty that forces their children to work. While we do this we are taking immediate action to make working conditions for youngsters like Rekha safer. As well as improving their access to vital healthcare, education and recreation.

10p a day can help stop a child having to work to survive

Just think what a month from you could do

4 Lots of direct appeals to the reader are used.

HIV/AIDS

£3 a month can help us protect HIV/AIDS orphans and children who are HIV positive. It can also support health education and stop more young people becoming infected with the virus.

Working children

£3 a month can help us fight the poverty which forces children to work. It can also give more working children the opportunity to go to school and the chance of a normal childhood.

Emergencies

£3 a month means we can be on hand whenever emergency strikes. Helping us bring aid to children in the poorest parts of the world – who have been robbed of almost everything by crisis.

- A donation every month will help us free children from poverty both now and in the future – in over 70 countries worldwide.

- A regular gift helps Save the Children give deprived families the skills and resources they need to build better lives.

- Every penny you give Save the Children makes a difference.

Please join us in partnership for the children

5 The ways in which the reader's money will help are explained many times.

Please support us with a gift of a month

Complete your monthly bankers order today. **Thank you.**

ERTY BEAT POVERTY BEAT POVERTY BEAT POVERTY BEAT POVERTY BEAT POVERTY BEAT POVERT

Save the Children

This is a web page from the Save the Children 'Beat Poverty' campaign.

1 The web page uses more graphics to interest the reader. On the web page these graphics are animated.

2 There is less text than on the leaflet.

3 The web page is not just asking for money.

4 Emotive language is still used but there is less of it: readers are already interested so need less persuading.

Unit 10 ◆ Understanding the influence of media texts

3 Work on your own. The paragraphs below compare how the Save the Children leaflet and the Beat Poverty website present the problems of child poverty. Read the first paragraph carefully. Then copy and complete the second paragraph about how the leaflet is designed to suit its audience.

> Save the Children is a charity that wants to get rid of child poverty. The charity uses different media to raise money and make people aware of the problem. The leaflet and website are two examples. They are quite different because the audience for each one is different.
>
> The audience for the leaflet is … The leaflet has to be very persuasive because … The leaflet uses many persuasive devices such as … Examples of this are …

4 Work on your own. Write a paragraph about the way the Beat Poverty website is designed to suit its audience. Use the paragraph you have just written about the leaflet to help you. You can add extra sentences if you need to. Use the sentence starter below to begin.

> The audience for the Beat Poverty website is different because …

5 Work as a class. Complete the tasks below.

1 First work on your own. Read your work very carefully.
   - Does it make sense and say what you meant it to say?
   - Have you used capital letters and full stops?
   - Have you used quotation marks around words you copied from the texts?
2 Now share your work with the class.
   - Pick out *two* good points about each student's paragraphs.
   - Identify *one* point the student could improve.

11 Explaining your point of view in detail

This unit will help you to:
- understand someone else's line of thought
- explain your point of view in standard Englis
- use connectives to show how ideas are linke
- write in complex sentences
- include different sorts of information in your writing

11.1 Understanding someone's line of thought

This section will help you to:
- understand someone's line of thought
- look at the way connectives show how ideas follow on from one another

 1 Work as a class. You are going to see how well you can use connectives.

1 Work in teams to play *Connective Bingo!*
- Your teacher will call out one of the connectives in the box below.
- Try to write down a sentence using that connective. If you do, cover the connective on the box below with a scrap of paper.
- The first team to cover all the connectives on their box wins.

| because | although | however | despite this | rather |
| instead | similarly | still | though | whereas |

2 Which of the connectives below have you met before? Use the hints to help you guess what they may mean.
- **a** nonetheless   (Hint: try breaking it up into three words)
- **b** furthermore   (Hint: try breaking it up into two words)
- **c** consequently   (Hint: what other word is it like?)

2 Work as a class. Read text A on the opposite page and look at the labels. Talk about how the connectives show readers the way the writer is thinking.

3 Work in pairs. Read memo B on the opposite page. Decide where Peter should use each of these connectives:

| furthermore | consequently | nonetheless |

A

Memo to Peter Shaw, Head of Programming, Your Choice TV

Re: Winter 2005, programme for the Saturday night 8.00–9.00pm slot

Over the summer the number of viewers on a Saturday night between 8.00pm and 9.00pm was very high. **Nonetheless**, we have to make sure the winter viewing figures are even better. **Consequently** choosing the right programme is vital. **Furthermore**, your Christmas bonus depends on the company making the right decision.

I look forward to receiving your detailed explanation of which programme we will be making for this slot.

Richard Mann

1 The point I just made is still true but this next point is more important.

2 Because of the last point I made you know this next point is true.

3 The point I am about to make adds to, and is even more important than, the last one.

B

Memo to Programme team, Your Choice TV

Re: Winter 2005, programme for the Saturday night 8.00–9.00pm slot

Our researchers have found that almost half the Saturday evening audience is aged under sixteen. _____ , we must not forget our older viewers. _____ , the programme we make must be geared to a family audience. _____ , we must be sure our programme will grab more viewers than any similar programmes on other TV channels.

Please bring all your detailed proposals to tomorrow's meeting.

Peter Shaw

4

Work as a pair. You are going to write down a formal, well argued discussion about which single change would really improve your school.

1 First practise your discussion in a role play. You are going to use connectives to link your ideas.

   a Read the instructions below. The speech bubbles show you how one pair of students did their role play.

   b Now decide who is going to be the student and who is going to be the school governor. Follow the instructions to have a formal discussion on how to improve your own school. Remember to:

   • speak in standard English

   • make sure that your ideas follow on from one another

   • use connectives to show how your ideas are linked.

Student: give your point of view about one thing which would really improve the school.

> Our school would be much better if students could choose what they wear.

Governor: suggest an improvement to the student's idea. Begin your point of view with **nonetheless**.

> **Nonetheless**, students' clothes would have to look smart and be clean.

Student: follow on by saying how the governor's idea could be made to work. Begin this point with **consequently**.

> **Consequently**, we could have a dress code so that, for example, dirty or torn jeans would not be allowed.

Governor: follow on by agreeing with the student's last point and adding another idea. Use the connective **furthermore**.

> **Furthermore**, we would still need to have rules about jewellery for safety reasons.

---

2 Now use what you have practised to write down a discussion in formal English using connectives.

5 **Work as a class. Share some of your formal discussions from activity 4.**

11.2 Working out your point of view

> **This section will help you to:**
> - take different pieces of information into account
> - use connectives to show your line of thought
> - explain your point of view in standard English

11.3 1 Work as a class.

1 Brainstorm *five* examples of standard and non-standard English. Write them in a chart like the one below.

Non-standard English	Standard English
He were took bad.	He was taken ill.
I ain't got it.	I do not have it.

2 Use standard English to talk about what sorts of television programmes appeal to:
- children aged 5–8
- teenagers
- adults aged 30–40
- families

Listen carefully to see if each of you is speaking in standard English.

2 Work as a class. Read about programmes A and B opposite.

1 Read the speech bubbles that show what Katie said at the meeting. Study how she uses the details to say how well the programme will appeal to a family audience.

2 Which comments should Katie change so that she is speaking in standard English? Decide what she should say instead.

3 Work in a group of three or four. Study programme suggestions C and D. Talk about how well each of them would suit a family audience. Check that each of you always speaks in standard English.

4 Work in a pair. Talk about programme suggestion E. How well would it suit a family audience? Make sure you speak in standard English.

5 Work as a class. Decide which programme Your Choice TV should make to appeal to a family audience. Listen carefully to each other and check you are all speaking in standard English.

Dear Programme Team

Please read these programme suggestions before the meeting. Come ready to discuss which is the best programme for Your Choice TV to make. Remember that we want a family audience.

Peter Shaw

Winter 2005:
Suggested programmes for
Saturday nights at 8.00pm

A *Ambulance!* A medical drama series which focuses on a middle-aged London ambulance crew. Drama comes from the emergency situations they have to deal with, as well as what is happening in their own lives.

B *The Spanners* A sit-com based around a family-owned garage in Liverpool. If there's a scam going the Spanners are in on it – but with disastrous and hilarious results.

C *Celebrity Charity Challenge* A game show where celebrity teams have to perform a task for charity. Tasks could include running a night shelter for the weekend, catching rare animals so they can be bred in zoos and saved, or taking aid to a remote Ethiopian village.

D *Crimewave* Young, good-looking Max Hammer is a local radio DJ. He finds himself turning into a detective when he uses his show to solve crimes for his listeners.

E *Sports Academy* Viewers choose ten hopeful athletes to go to Sports Academy. There they are coached by experts and use superb training facilities. Each Saturday they face a sporting challenge, and viewers vote to decide who will leave the academy. The overall winner wins a year's sponsorship and may be picked for the Olympic team.

1 This might not appeal to younger viewers.

2 They're cool to watch.

3 If it's about a family it might appeal to families.

4 Women might find a programme set in a garage dead boring.

5 Viewers all likes a good laugh.

11.3

Using complex sentences to express your ideas

This section will help you to:
- use a variety of connectives in your writing
- write complex sentences
- write in a suitably formal way

1 Work as a class. Look back at the work you did on complex sentences in Units 2 and 9. Read the chart below. It shows how you can recognise different sorts of sentences. Then do the work below the chart.

Type of sentence	How it is built	Example
Simple sentence	It has one **main clause**. A main clause is a group of words that makes sense on its own.	I enjoy watching *Casualty*.
Compound sentence	It is made up of **two or more main clauses** joined with one of these connectives: **and, or, but**	I enjoy watching *Casualty* but I prefer watching a film.
Complex sentence	It has two different sorts of clauses: **a main clause and a subordinate clause**. A subordinate clause does not make sense on its own. It needs to be joined to a main clause to make sense. It starts with a connective such as: **because, although, if, when, since, so, while, after, unless** When the subordinate clause comes first, a comma is usually used before the main clause.	I always watch a film when there's one on. If there's no film on, I enjoy watching *Casualty*.

1 Read sentences **A–D**. Decide what type of sentence each one is. Hint: work out what sorts of clauses make up the sentence.

A My brother teases me because I like *Friends* so much.

B A girl in my class has all the *Friends* videos.

C If I am out, Dad records *Friends* for me.

D The last series was good but the latest one is even better.

2 Work as a class. Read the text below. People often use complex sentences when they write in a formal way. Find out how a writer used complex sentences to write about the views of this group of teenagers. Then do the work below.

> I don't mind watching a programme about celebrities. It's got to have music as well.
> **Liam**

> I enjoy watching a music chart show. I like watching the videos.
> **Rashid**

> I don't want to watch sport on a Saturday night. It's really boring.
> **Polly**

1 Instead of shortened words like 'don't,' the writer used 'does not' to make it sound more formal.

Polly does not want to watch sport on a Saturday night because she finds it boring.

Rashid enjoys watching a music chart show since he likes watching the videos.

Liam does not mind watching a programme about celebrities if it has music as well.

2 The writer used a connective to help turn what each teenager said into a complex sentence.

1 Read what Su Lin said. Work out how to write her ideas as one complex sentence.

> I like watching teenagers acting in a soap. The plot needs to be really exciting.
> **Su Lin**

3 **Work in pairs. Add a subordinate clause to complete each of these complex sentences. Use the connective in brackets.**

> **A** Some people enjoy watching football on Saturday night
>
> _____ . (although)
>
> **B** Young children really enjoy watching cartoon films
>
> _____ . (because)
>
> **C** (Unless) _____ ,
>
> I usually watch a pop music programme.
>
> **D** (While) _____ ,
>
> we sometimes share a packet of crisps.

4 **Work in a group of three or four.**

> **1** Talk about which *three* TV programmes you like to watch on a Saturday night if you are staying in. Give reasons for your view.
>
> **2** Now work on your own. Write *three* complex sentences in standard English explaining your point of view.
>
> - Remember not to use shortened words.
> - Use one of the connectives in the box in each sentence.
>
> | because | although | if | when | since | so |
> |---------|----------|-----|------|-------|-----|

5 **Work in pairs.**

> **1** Read and mark each other's complex sentences in standard English.
>
> - Tick each sentence that makes sense.
> - Underline the main clause in each sentence.
> - Put a circle around the subordinate clause.
> - Put a cross by any shortened words.
>
> **2** Explain to the rest of the class how you made *one* of your complex sentences.

Writing about different sorts of information

This section will help you to:
- write about different sorts of information
- make sure your text is easy to follow
- explain your point of view clearly and in detail

11.4 1 **Work as a class.**

1 Read the words in the box. They are used to describe different numbers of something.

> few   fewer   most   more   fewest   similar   equal

2 Now draw a line like the one below. Decide where each word should fit on it:

⟵——————————————————— *fewer* ———————————⟶

3 Copy and complete this chart. Then write *two* sentences about the survey. Use words from the list above.

	Boys		Girls	
	Yes	No	Yes	No
Did you watch television for more than three hours last night?				

2 **Work as a class. You are going to write about the results of a survey.**

1 Rob's class carried out a survey about television viewing. Rob had to write about the survey results for homework. Read his first paragraph opposite. Look at the labels to see how he turned the information in the table into text.

2 Use the information on the second row of the chart to write the second paragraph.

3 **Work as a pair. Write the third paragraph using the information from the third and fourth rows of the chart opposite.**

4 **Work on your own. Write a paragraph about the information in the fifth row of the chart.**

Writing about different sorts of information

	Boys (15 in class)	Girls (15 in class)	Rob (Why?)
1 Number of hours spent watching television (average)	4	3	Two hours – I prefer playing with my Playstation. On Saturday I watch more because there is sport on.
2 Favourite comedian	Lenny Henry (10) Dawn French (5)	Dawn French (12) Lenny Henry (3)	Lenny Henry because he pretends to be lots of really funny people.
3 Favourite soap	*EastEnders* (7) *Neighbours* (7) None (1)	*EastEnders* (3) *Neighbours* (12)	I never watch soaps because I don't enjoy them.
4 Number of soaps watched each week (average)	2	4	0
5 Most popular type of film	Thrillers (15)	Thrillers (4) Love stories (11)	I like thrillers because they're very exciting.

1 The first sentence tells readers what the information is about.

2 Numbers are written as words.

> Rob Sadler   Class 9C's television survey
> Everyone in my class enjoys watching television every day.
> The boys watch <u>more</u> television because they watch about
> four hours of television each day whereas the girls only
> watch three hours. I watch for fewer hours than most people
> because I prefer playing on my Playstation. Nonetheless
> I still watch two hours most days and more on a Saturday
> when I watch 'Grandstand'.

3 The writer uses connectives to:
- compare different pieces of information (*whereas*)
- introduce a reason (*because*)
- add a further point (*nonetheless*)

4 Titles of programmes are put inside inverted commas (' ') in handwriting. (In print they are usually in *italics*.)

5 Work in pairs. Mark each other's paragraphs.

- Circle all the numbers that are written in words.
- Tick programme titles with inverted commas round them.
- Underline the different connectives your partner used.

12 Reaching a sensible conclusion

This unit will help you to:
- compare different points of view
- discuss pieces of evidence that do not agree
- reach a sensible conclusion
- write a balanced analysis of a situation

12.1 Comparing different points of view

This section will help you to:
- understand different points of view
- recognise what is similar and what is different in two points of view
- decide how important these differences are

1 Work as a class.

1 Talk about what an opinion is. How can you tell the difference between a fact and an opinion?

2 You are going to find out how to compare different opinions. First read the box below.

Mr Phillips' decision

Mr Phillips has the money to buy one PC game for the school's Learning Resource Centre. He wants to choose a game that the students will enjoy, but he also has his own opinions about which games are suitable. He has looked at lots of games, and now he has to choose between these two.

Solve It – a game based on the popular Ewan Klew's detective novels. Players have to find and examine different types of evidence to solve crimes and mysteries based on the novels. The game uses accurate information from science, geography and maths, and also from police work. It has five levels of difficulty.

Napoleon – A game based on the wars fought by the French leader Napoleon when he tried to conquer the world about two hundred years ago. It uses accurate information from history and geography. Players choose a country, train their army and try to beat Napoleon before he conquers them.

2 Work as a class. You are going to find out how Mr Phillips should go about making a sensible decision.

> 1 Study the three steps below. Look at how the chart below has been filled in using the first paragraph of Mr Phillips' opinion opposite.
>
> 2 Now make a chart like the one below. Practise using the steps. Read the second paragraph of Mr Phillips' opinion. Compare his opinion with that of the students.

How to compare two opinions and decide whether differences are important

Step 1 Read a paragraph of Mr Phillips' opinion carefully. Note each of the points he makes in column 1 of your chart.

Step 2 Look at each of Mr Phillips' points in turn. Scan the students' opinion to see if it agrees or disagrees with the point you're studying. Note what the second opinion says in column 2 or 3.

Step 3 Decide which points on your chart are most important. Put a star by:

- Mr Phillips' points – his point of view will be important because he's got the final choice.

- Any points students make that show they learn information or a skill through playing a PC game – this is important because the game will be used in a Learning Resource Centre.

Mr Phillips' opinion	Students' opinion	
	Agree	Disagree
* Lines 1–6: He likes games based on good books, like 'Lord of the Rings'.		Lines 7–8: They like games based on a film plot or science fiction games.

3 Work in pairs. Search the third paragraph of Mr Phillips' opinion. Follow the three steps again to compare his opinions with those of the students.

4 Work as a class. Use the stars on your charts to help you make a list of the features Mr Phillips should look for in a PC game. Keep this list to help you do the rest of the work in this unit.

Different people's opinions about PC games

Mr Phillips' opinion

When I'm choosing a game for the Learning Resource Centre I often look for one based on a good book such as *Lord of the Rings* or *Harry Potter and the Philosopher's Stone*. Students can compare what happens in the
5 game with the story in the book. Playing the game might even encourage students to read the book.

I also look for games where students have to solve a puzzle or use information in different ways. If a game has a historical setting then the information in it must
10 be accurate.

I know the graphics and a high speed of play are really important to the students, so I look at those things carefully too. I prefer games that have multiplay rather than just single play because then students have to
15 work together. I don't want to buy racing or sports games because students can play those at home – they don't learn anything by playing them.

The students' opinion

We love PC games about sports like football or motor racing – Formula One and rally games are both cool. We just love competing with our mates, so the game must have really good speed of play.

5 We also like games where there are puzzles to solve and lots of different levels to reach. As long as the graphics are good, we enjoy science fiction games and games that are based on the story of a film. We find games where you just do something like build a film
10 set and design the characters to make a film pretty boring. However, if it's building a real place in history and then carrying out the battles, that can be good fun.

5 **Work in pairs. Take it in turns to explain how you compared two opinions.**

We found ...

Then ... searched ...

12.2

Reaching a sensible conclusion

This section will help you to:
- discuss different pieces of evidence
- decide how important a difference is
- reach a sensible conclusion

1

Work as a class.

1 Talk about the information in the chart below. Is it fact or opinion?

2 Study the chart and answer these questions.

    a Which features do both games have?

    b Which features does only *Solve It* have?

    c Which features does only *Napoleon* have?

Features of PC games	*Solve It*	*Napoleon*
1 Good graphics	✓	✓
2 High speed of play	✗	✓
3 Multiplay	✓	✓
4 Create characters	✓	✗
5 Sport-based game	✗	✗
6 Game based on a film	✗	✗
7 Game based on a story	✓	✗
8 Different levels to reach	✓	✗
9 Puzzles to solve	✓	✓
10 Battles to fight	✗	✓
11 Racing game	✗	✗
12 Real places /times	✗	✓
13 Accurate information	✓	✓

3 Look back at your list of features that Mr Phillips should look for from page 129.

    a Which of the features does *Solve It* have?

    b Which of the features does *Napoleon* have?

evidence – the information you will use to help you make your decision. This information can be made up of *facts* and *opinions*.

2 **Work as a class. First read the key term box above. Then do the tasks below.**

1 Study the steps below to see how important the first difference in the chart is.

2 Practise the three steps as you look at the next difference between the games.

Features of PC games	*Solve It*	*Napoleon*
1 Good graphics	✓	✓
2 High speed of play	✗	✓
3 Multiplay	✓	✓
4 Create characters	✓	✗

Deciding how important differences in evidence are

Step 1 Look at the facts about the two games. Find a place where the evidence is different:

Napoleon *has high speed of play but* Solve It *does not.*

Step 2 Compare the difference with your list of features the game must have:

High speed of play is on the list. It is an important feature if a game will be used in the Learning Resource Centre.

Step 3 Ask: Does it matter that this piece of evidence is different?

Yes, so this is one advantage that Napoleon *has over* Solve It.

3 Work in a group of three or four. Study rows 5–8 of the chart on page 131. Use the three steps and work out what advantages and disadvantages each game has.

4 Work on your own. Study rows 9–13 of the chart. Use the three steps again. Work out what advantages and disadvantages each game has.

5 Work as a class.

1 Talk about the advantages and disadvantages of each game. Which game has the most advantages? Which game should Mr Phillips choose for the Learning Resource Centre?

2 Talk together about:
   • how you compared different pieces of evidence
   • how you decided which pieces of evidence really mattered
   • how you went about reaching a sensible conclusion.

12.3

Planning to write a balanced analysis

This section will help you to:
- understand how an analysis text is written
- write about different sorts of evidence
- balance different opinions and evidence
- write a plan for a balanced analysis of a situation

1 Work as a class. You are going to find out how an analysis text is written.

> **1** Study the words in the box below. Talk about what each one means.
>
> | | | | |
> |---|---|---|---|
> | answer | evidence | opinion | compares |
> | fact | advantages | disadvantages | question |

Key term

analysis – a text that looks at the key features of something and discusses how important they are

2 Work as a class. Read the key term box above. Now read each paragraph of the analysis text below and opposite. It was written by the leader of a Youth Club. The labels explain the job each part of the text does. Use words from the box above to complete them.

```
Which PC game should the Youth Club buy?

The Youth Club has enough funds to buy one
more PC game. Members of the Youth Club have
suggested that we buy either Oscar or Space
War. In order to decide which game is most
5  suitable, I will consider the opinions of the
members and the other youth leaders. I will
also compare the features of the two PC games.

Youth Club members feel that the most important
features in a PC game are good graphics and
10 speed of play. Members enjoy playing games
```

A Title – *says what*
q_____ the
writer is trying to
answer.

B Introduction – *The*
writer explains what
they are trying to work
out and what sort of
_____ is going to
be looked at.

where they have to solve puzzles and go up
levels of difficulty. They also prefer games
which involve racing or battling against each
other. Similarly the youth leaders agree that
15 good graphics, high speed of play, puzzles to
solve and levels to go through are important.
However, they also thought that games should be
multiplay, straightforward to learn, and not be
violent.

20 The two games are quite different. In **Oscar** you
have to create a film producer who has to solve
different puzzles to get the film finished and
win an Oscar. The game has excellent graphics
and can be played in single or multiplay. Also
25 it is straightforward to learn and play, so all
the Youth Club members could use it. In
contrast **Space War** is a science fiction game.
Players have to blow up each other's
spaceships, which means that the game is mildly
30 violent. In addition, some of its instructions
are quite difficult to follow. However, the
graphics are excellent, the game has puzzles to
solve and its high speed of play makes it very
enjoyable to play.

35 Both **Space War** and **Oscar** have excellent
graphics, puzzle-solving games and multiplay,
which both members and the youth leaders prefer.
Although it is true that **Space War** may get
played more than **Oscar** by those members who can
40 understand the instructions, the game has an
important disadvantage. **Space War** contains mild
violence, which is a feature the youth leaders
want to avoid in PC games. By contrast **Oscar** is
not at all violent. In addition, all members of
45 the Youth Club will be able to understand the
instructions for **Oscar** and play it, which is
also important to the youth leaders.

Having examined what the games offer and the
opinions of Youth Club members and the youth
50 leaders, I have decided that the best PC game
to buy is **Oscar**. This is both because it is
free from any violence and because all Youth
Club members will be able to enjoy its
excellent graphics, high speed of play and
55 puzzle-solving games.

C Paragraph 1 – *The writer compares the _____ of the members and youth leaders.*

D Paragraph 2 – *The writer _____ the _____ about the two games.*

E Paragraph 3 – *The writer explains what _____ and _____ each game has.*

F Conclusion – *The writer explains what is a reasonable _____ to the question.*

3 Work as a class. You have just seen what an analysis text is like. You are going to write an analysis to help Mr Phillips decide on a PC game. Now copy and complete the first four rows of the chart below. Answer the questions and write a plan for your own analysis.

Plan	Notes
Title What question sums up what you're trying to work out?	Which PC game should Mr Phillips buy for …
Introduction • What are you trying to find out? • What evidence are you going to look at? • What is each game about?	Mr Phillips can choose one game for the … Mr Phillip's opinions and … *Solve It* is … *Napoleon* is …
Paragraph 1: Compare people's opinions Use the chart you made earlier • Which points do Mr Phillips and the students agree about? • Which points do Mr Phillips and the students disagree about?	
Paragraph 2: Compare the information about the games Which features of the games are: • the same? • different?	
Paragraph 3: Explain what advantages and disadvantages each game has • What advantages does each game have? • What disadvantages does each game have?	
Conclusion: Decide what the answer to your question is • Which PC game should Mr Phillips choose? Why?	

4 Work as a pair. Complete the chart for paragraph 3 and the conclusion.

5 Work as a class. Without using your notes, discuss what sort of information you put in each of the six boxes of your plan.

12.4 Making clear how your ideas are linked

This section will help you to:
- use connectives to show how points are linked
- explain how your ideas are linked
- write a balanced analysis of a situation

1 **Work as a class. Read the analysis text on pages 134 and 135 again.**

1 List the connectives the writer used to link points.

2 Sort these connectives into three groups:
- connectives that show that points agree: *and, also*
- connectives that show that points disagree: *however…*
- connectives that show that points are balanced against each other.

2 **Work as a class.**

1 Study the examples opposite of how points can be linked together.

2 Study the pairs of points below. Then write each pair out using the best connective from your lists above to show readers how they link.

> **A** • Mr Phillips prefers games where students have to use information in different ways.
> • Students are more interested in games where you can go up to different levels.

> **B** • Mr Phillips wants the graphics and speed of play in a game to be good.
> • Students think excellent graphics and high speed of play make games more enjoyable.

> **C** • Students love competing with each other in PC games about motor racing.
> • Mr Phillips thinks students can play motor racing games at home.

Using connectives to show how points are linked

A Points that agree

- Mr Phillips likes games where there are puzzles to solve.
- The students enjoy solving puzzles in PC games.

Mr Phillips likes games where you have to solve puzzles. **Similarly** the students enjoy solving puzzles in PC games.

1 This connective is used before the next point to show readers it agrees with the point made in the last sentence.

B Points that disagree

- Mr Phillips prefers PC games based on good books.
- The students would rather have a PC game based on a film.

Mr Phillips prefers PC games based on good books. **However**, the students would rather have a PC game based on a film.

2 This connective shows readers the next point disagrees with the previous one.

C Points that balance

- Students love games based on sports or where they have to race one another.
- Mr Phillips dislikes sports and race games because he thinks students do not learn anything by playing them.

On the one hand students love games based on sports or where they have to race one another. **On the other hand** Mr Phillips dislikes sports and race games because he thinks students do not learn anything by playing them.

3 These connectives tell readers that the writer is balancing the points in these sentences against each other.

3 Work in a group of three or four. Link pairs of points together using the best connective from your lists to show how they link. Find one pair that agree, one pair that disagree and one pair that balance.

> A Both games have good graphics and involve puzzles.
>
> B *Solve It* is based on a well known series of stories.
>
> C In *Solve It* players can solve crimes and mysteries.
>
> D The two games use accurate information.
>
> E In *Napoleon* players fight battles.
>
> F *Napoleon* is based on a real time and place.

4 Work in pairs. Which of these points should be linked? Find one pair that agree, one pair that disagree and one pair that balance. Write out your answer using connectives to show how the points link.

> A Neither game involves sport or racing.
>
> B In *Solve It* students can enjoy going up different levels.
>
> C In *Napoleon* there is only one level of play.
>
> D Playing *Solve It* and *Napoleon* will help students learn.
>
> E An advantage of *Napoleon* is its high speed of play.
>
> F A disadvantage of *Solve It* is that it does not have high speed of play.

12.6 **5** Work as a class.

> 1 Share the pairs of points you have made and the connectives you have used to link them.
>
> 2 Use the plan you made on page 136 and the points you have linked above to write a complete analysis text.

13 Preparing for the reading test

This unit will help you to:
- work out what sort of answer a question is looking for
- understand how to answer different types of questions
- write a detailed answer using quotations

13.1 Understanding the question

This section will help you to:
- work out what a question is asking you to do

13.1 1   Work as a class.

> 1 Brainstorm what you should do when you are first given your test paper.
>
> > *Read the instructions …*
>
> 2 Read Question 1 on the opposite page and look at the labels around it. Talk about what you have to do to answer this question.

2   Work as a class. It is important to understand exactly what a test question means. The words in the box below are taken from the test questions on the opposite page. Find where each word is used and talk about what it means.

> explain   emphasises   phrase   conveys   attitude   contrast

When you explain something, you give reasons for it.

3   Work in pairs. Read Questions 2 and 3 opposite carefully. Then decide what sort of information you should give for each one.

> *In Question 2 you must say how the sentence shows …*

4   Work on your own. Read Questions 4 and 5 opposite carefully. Then decide for each one what sort of information you should give.

5   Work as a class. Share your answers to activity 4. Talk about what you must do to answer a test question well.

1 This tells you where to look for the information.

2 This tells you what information to look for.

3 This tells you which event you're looking for.

4 Write each piece of information on a new line.

5 You need to give both pieces of information to get full marks.

Question 1 From the second paragraph, write down the day and exact time of the aeroplane crash.

- _____

- _____

(1 mark)

Question 2 Explain how the writer emphasises Tom's feelings in the third sentence:

'Feeling rather anxious, Tom waited for the plane to arrive.'

- _____

_____

(1 mark)

Question 3 Complete the chart below, giving TWO advantages and ONE disadvantage of keeping animals in zoos. (2 marks)

Advantages	Disadvantage
1	1
2	

Question 4 The writer contrasts the power of the tiger with the fear of the crowd. Pick out two phrases that show this contrast.

Power   **Fear**

- _____   - _____

(2 marks)

Question 5 Find and copy an adjective in the text that conveys the writer's attitude towards the tiger. Explain what the attitude is.

- _____

- _____

(2 marks)

Finding information in a text

This section will help you answer questions that ask you to:
• find information

 1 Work as a class. Share your answers to these questions.

1 How do you work out what a question is asking you to do?
First read the question carefully. Look for …

2 What do you do when you scan a text? What do you do differently when you skim?

3 What should you do if you don't understand a word or sentence in a text?

> Re-read the bit …

2 Work as a class. Read the text opposite. Use the labels to help you answer Question 6 by scanning the text.

Question 6   Who was the first person to bottle food?   (1 mark)

3 Work as a group. Use skimming and scanning to help you answer these questions about the text opposite.

Question 7   Why was Napoleon interested in preserving food? (1 mark)
Question 8   What food did the French Navy order from Appert?(1 mark)
Question 9   When did Donkin and Hall start canning food?   (1 mark)
Question 10 Which material did Donkin and Hall use to make food containers?   (1 mark)

4 Work on your own. Use skimming and scanning to help you answer these questions about the text opposite.

Question 11 Which members of the Royal family first ate canned beef?   (1 mark)
Question 12 Where did Admiral Ross take cans of food?   (1 mark)
Question 13 How long after Napoleon offered his prize could people in England buy canned food in the shops? (1 mark)

1 I had to answer this question: 'Who was the first person to bottle food?' I needed to find and copy the name.

2 I ran my finger along each line of text searching for the key words 'bottle' and 'food'. The person who did this bottling is a 'he'. I looked back to an earlier sentence to find his name: Nicholas Appert.

The history of the food can

In 1795 Napoleon, the French leader, was trying to conquer Europe, but his soldiers and sailors were dying from hunger and from eating bad food. Therefore he offered a prize of 12,000 francs to anyone who could find a reliable way to preserve food. Nicholas
5 Appert, a chef and winemaker from Paris, was determined to win this prize. After years of experimentation, he found that if he sealed cooked food in bottles and stood them in boiling water, the food did not go off. He set up the first food-bottling plant and sold his products at a shop at 8, rue Boucher, in Paris. The French Navy
10 placed its first official order in 1807, and bottled beans, soups and peas were taken on board ships going to the Caribbean.

In 1810 Appert's ideas were taken up in England by Peter Durand, who had the idea of using tinplate containers instead of glass. The seal was more reliable, and the cans were stronger than glass
15 bottles. Bryan Donkin and John Hall, who knew all about tinplate, set up a commercial canning factory in 1813 and sent cans of their preserved beef to the Royal family. It met with Royal approval and was given the first Royal testimonial, which said that the patent beef had been placed: '... on the Duke of York's table where it was
20 tasted by the Queen, the Prince Regent and several distinguished personages and highly approved.'

Within a year, canned foods were taken on board Admiral Ross's ships bound for the Arctic. The Royal Navy was a good customer, placing such huge orders that it was not until 1830 that canned
25 foods were first on sale in the shops. Initially the shops only sold sardines, tomatoes and peas. Cans of food were expensive and, because can-openers hadn't been invented, people had to use chisels and hammers to open them.

 5 Work as a class. Talk about the best ways to answer a question that asks you to find information.

Reading between the lines

This section will help you answer questions that ask you to:
- work out what a writer is suggesting or hinting at

 1 **Work as a class. Read the text opposite. Then talk about how you work out what a writer is hinting at.**

First look at the detail …

2 **Work as a class. Questions that ask you to read between the lines may use one of these words: *hint, suggest, imply, convey, indicate*. The example below shows you how to answer a question that asks you to read between the lines.**

> **Question 1** What do these sentences suggest about what Dad is feeling?
>
> Still Dad said nothing. He smiled determinedly, but he didn't hum. He didn't even tap his fingers on the steering-wheel. (1 mark)

> **Step 1: Search each sentence. What does each detail suggest?**
> - *'smiles determinedly' shows his smile isn't real*
> - *'but he didn't hum' means he isn't happy*
> - *'even' shows he isn't behaving like his usual self.*
>
> **Step 2: In your answer explain what the details showed you.**
>
> *The word 'determinedly' shows that Dad is forcing himself to smile …*

3 **Work in pairs. Work out a detailed answer to this question.**

> **Question 2** Read lines 1–2. How is Vee feeling? (1 mark)

4 **Work on your own to answer this question.**

> **Question 3** Read lines 9–19. What does Freda's behaviour on arrival at the cottage suggest about her? (1 mark)

5 **Work as a class. Talk about:**
- how you spotted that a question wants you to read between the lines
- how you worked out what the writer was hinting at.

Dad is driving his daughter Vee and her stepmother Freda far out into the countryside. His passengers have no idea where they are going. They hope they are going to a luxury hotel for the next part of their English holiday.

'Dad!' Vee said. 'We've had enough of this! Tell us where we're going, *please!*'

Still Dad said nothing. He smiled determinedly, but he didn't hum. He didn't even tap his fingers on the steering-wheel. They drove up
5 between the trees. Soon the valley could be seen beneath them, and so could a network of other dirt tracks with dots of cottages on them. Vee hoped that they were on a way back out of the valley, but suddenly she saw a chimney up ahead. A gate appeared between the trees, leading into a garden. Dad turned the car through the
10 gate, and Vee found herself staring at a cottage.

She was never to forget the first time she saw its old, leaded windows, candy-twist chimneys, crumbling front porch and wooden shack of a garage – into which Dad now, **proprietorially**, drew the hire car. He turned off the engine and Freda leapt out.
15 Wobbling slightly on her high heels, she pronounced that it was a dear little cottage, and she really didn't mind that it wasn't a grand hotel. A quaint country bed-and-breakfast place would do just as well. She began to hurry towards the crumbling porch, declaring that she couldn't wait to find her room and take a shower.

20 Dad tried to call her back, but she was gone already, ringing on the bell and calling for assistance with the luggage in the car.

'There must be some mistake,' Vee said.

Dad produced a key. It wasn't a holiday-cottage key with the owner's name attached, and instructions about when to drop it off
25 when their week was done. It was on a key-ring which bore Dad's name. JAMES VAN PRAGUE.

'There's no mistake,' Dad said. 'I signed the lease for it this morning. We've got it for the next ninety-nine years. This is Caus Cottage. Our home.'

Taken from *The Candle House* by Pauline Fisk

proprietorially – behaving like the owner would

13.4

Writing about the way a text is organised

This section will help you answer questions about how a writer:
- has made the text look
- has used paragraphs
- has used different types of sentences

 1 Work as a class. Read the text opposite. To answer a question about how a text is organised, first work out what job the whole text is doing. Ask:
- what **type** of text it is: *First it explains why ..., then it ...*
- who the text is meant for (the **audience**): *people who ...*
- why the writer has written this text (its **purpose**).

2 Work as a class. Follow the two steps below to answer Question 1.

> **Question 1** Why does the first paragraph start with a question?   (1 mark)

> **Step 1 Ask: What job is the part you are asked about doing?**
> *This first paragraph explains why Ainsley Harriott wrote the book.*
>
> **Step 2 Ask: How does the feature you're asked about help the text (or this part of it) do its job?**
> *Using a question makes the reader want to read on to find the answer. It also tells the reader what the paragraph is about – it answers this question.*

3 Work in pairs. Use the two steps to help you answer this question.

> **Question 2** Why have italics been used in the first sentence of the second paragraph?   (1 mark)

4 Work on your own. Use the two steps to answer this question.

> **Question 3** Why have questions been used in paragraph 3?   (1 mark)

5 Work as a class. Answer Question 4 together.

> **Question 4** In what ways is the last sentence an effective way to end this introduction?   (2 marks)

introduction

So ... why meals in minutes? Well, the amount of times people
have come up to me, especially in supermarkets, occasionally in
the dry cleaner's, now and then in the florist's and also in the
Gent's, and asked me to recommend a delicious recipe that can
5 be knocked up in minutes rather than hours is quite
staggering! I discovered that these people all had something in
common: some worked strange shifts, some were loaded with
children, but generally it was a case of working hard and
playing hard, yet everyone wanted to eat fantastic home-
10 cooked food in a flash. So, I wanted to write a book and make
a television series that would hopefully give them food for thought and
answer all those **culinary conundrums**. And here it is!

Believe me, once you get into *Meals in Minutes* your enthusiasm for good,
simple nosh becomes more and more infectious. You'll be able to bounce
15 into your kitchen knowing that whatever is hanging around can be quickly
whipped into a gourmet feast. Food shopping will be done with
confidence – invaluable if you're stretched for time. Just think, you'll be
able to pick up a few ingredients, fresh or ready-made, knowing that
they'll combine beautifully with all those store-cupboard goodies at home.

20 Now, just because food is cooked in minutes instead of hours doesn't
mean you have to compromise on great taste and presentation – even
with classics like my Coq au Vin or Cassoulet, or, indeed, my 20-minute
Peking Duck. They all look fabulous and taste wonderful. Perhaps you're
looking for a complete roast dinner in less than an hour, or stunning
25 snacks in five minutes flat. Yes, there's not a lot you can do in five
minutes in the kitchen is there? Feeling smart? How's about breathtaking
dazzling desserts like my Zapped Lemon Curd Pudding or my Choco-nana
Brandy Snaps, both ready in less than twelve minutes? Oooh you lucky
people. Go on, get into meals in minutes, discover the art of the perfect
30 store-cupboard, lots of brilliant kitchen tips and fast, fabulous food.

Enjoy!

Taken from *Meals in Minutes*
by Ainsley Harriott

culinary conundrums – questions about cooking

13.5 Writing about the way a writer uses language

> **This section will help you answer questions where you have to:**
> • explain how a writer has used language in an effective way

 1 **Work as a class. You are going to talk about language features.**

1 Use the terms in the box to complete the definitions below.

> alliteration   simile

> **A** A _____ is a word picture (image) that is a comparison
> using the words 'like' or 'as': *Ruins like crumbling hands; fierce as a lion.*
>
> **B** _____ is when words near each other begin with the
> same sound: *puffing and panting.*

2 Read the text below, then answer this question.

> **Question 1** Find one example of each of these in the text.
> a) alliteration   b) simile   (1 mark)

> Like a giant corkscrew, the stairway twisted through the
> darkness, steep and narrow and with no rail to guide them.
> The wind howled cruelly in an effort to tear them loose,
> and the fog dragged clammy fingers down their backs; but
> 5   up the giddy flight they went, each one helping the others,
> until at last the clouds parted, the darkness fell away, and
> a glow of golden sunrays warmed their arrival. The castle
> gate swung smoothly open, and on a rug as soft as a
> snowdrift they entered the great hall and they stood
> 10   shyly waiting.
>
> Taken from *The Phantom Tollbooth* by Norton Juster

2 Work as a class. Study the example below. It shows you how to answer a question on the way a writer uses language.

> **Question 2** How does the writer's use of language in the first sentence of the passage opposite convey the difficulty of climbing the stairs? (1 mark)

> **Step 1 What is the writer showing you?**
> *It is difficult because the stairs are twisted, steep and narrow, and ...*
>
> **Step 2 Which parts of the description work really well? Why?**
> *'Like a giant corkscrew' suggests that the staircase is steep and tightly curved. This would make it very difficult to climb.*
>
> **Step 3 Now write your answer. Remember to:**
> • use quotations
> • make sure that the point you are making answers the question.
> *The simile 'Like a giant corkscrew' suggests that the staircase is steep and tightly curved, which would make it hard to climb.*

3 Work in pairs. Read the passage again. Answer these questions.

> **Question 3** What does the phrase 'the fog dragged clammy fingers down their backs' suggest? (1 mark)
>
> **Question 4** What does the word 'shyly' tell the reader about the characters? (1 mark)

4 Work on your own. Answer Question 5.

> **Question 5** What does the phrase 'as soft as a snowdrift' in the final sentence suggest about the rug? (1 mark)

5 Work as a class. Share your answers to Questions 3–5. Then work together to answer Question 6. (Hint: 'tone' means mood or feeling.)

> **Question 6** How does the tone of the passage change in line 6? Support your answer with two quotations. (1 mark)

13.6 Writing about the whole text

This section will help you write answers where you need to:
- explain what a writer has achieved in a text

 1 Work as a class. Read the text opposite. Decide what is:
- its genre or text type
- its intended audience
- its purpose.

2 Work as a class. Read Question 1 about the whole text. Find out how to answer it by following the steps below.

> **Question 1** How has Bill Bryson made his description entertaining? You should consider:
> - how he describes the hut
> - his description of what happens once they settle down to sleep
> - how the two men are shown to react
> - the way the writer has used language. (5 marks)

Step 1 Make sure you understand what the question asks you to do:
Write about each bullet point explaining what makes the text entertaining.

Step 2 Search the text for details you can write about for each point:
- how he describes the hut

  The hut is 'dark and leaky', 'like chocolate pudding' ...

Step 3 Use the details you picked out to answer the question:
The way the hut is described is entertaining because Bill Bryson makes it sound such an awful place to stay. He says it is 'dark and leaky' and compares the mud floor to 'chocolate pudding' which suggests it's all sticky. He tells you just how dirty it is with its 'cramped and filthy sleeping platform', and 'wet litter'. There is even water everywhere. No one would want to stay there, but Bryson and Katz have to, so it's fun to read about what happens to them.

---

3 Work as a class. Follow the steps and write about the second bullet point in the question.

 4 Work on your own. Follow the steps and write about the third and fourth bullet points in the question.

 5 Work as a class. Share your answers to activities 3 and 4.

IW
p.189

Travel writer Bill Bryson has set out with Stephen Katz to walk the longest footpath in the world, called the Appalachian Trail. Tonight they have to sleep in one of the mountain shelters along the way.

The interior was <u>dark and leaky</u>, with a <u>mud floor like chocolate pudding</u>, a <u>cramped and filthy sleeping platform</u>, and scraps of <u>wet litter</u> everywhere. <u>Water ran down the inside of the walls and trickled into pools on the sleeping ledge.</u> Outside there was <u>no picnic table</u>, as at most other shelters, and <u>no privy</u>. Even by the **austere** standards of the Appalachian Trail, <u>this was grim</u>.

5

… I had a look at the shelter register while Katz boiled water for noodles. Every shelter has a register in which visitors make diary-like entries on the weather or their state of mind, if any, and note any unusual occurrences. This one mentioned only a couple of odd bearlike noises outside in the night, but what really caught the attention of the shelter's **chroniclers** was the unusual liveliness of its resident mice and even rats, and this, I can now **attest,** was so.

10

From the moment – the moment – we put our heads down that night there were the scurryings and scutterings of rodents. They were absolutely fearless and scampered freely over our bags and even across our heads. Cursing furiously, Katz banged around at them with his water bottle and whatever else came to hand. Once I turned on my headlamp to find a packmouse on top of my sleeping bag, high up on my chest, not six inches from my chin, sitting up on its haunches, and regarding me with a **gimlet** eye. **Reflexively**, I hit the bag from inside, flipping him into startled **oblivion**.

15

'Got one!' cried Katz.

20

'Me, too,' I said, rather proudly.

Katz was scrabbling around on his hands and knees as if trying to pass for a mouse himself, enlivening the dark with a flying flashlight beam and pausing from time to time to hurl a boot or bang down his water bottle. Then he would crawl back into his bag, be still for a time, curse abruptly, fling off **encumbrances** and repeat the process. I buried myself in my bag and pulled the drawstring tight over my head. And thus passed the night, with repeated sequences of Katz being violent, followed by silence, followed by scamperings, followed by Katz being violent. I slept surprisingly well, all things considered.

25

Taken from *A Walk in the Woods* by Bill Bryson

austere – lacking any comforts
chroniclers – people who write down what happens
attest – declare to be true
gimlet – something piercing
reflexively – without stopping to think
oblivion – unconsciousness or death
encumbrances – things that get in the way

14 Preparing for the writing test

14.1 Understanding the question

This section will help you to:
• work out what a question is asking you to do

1 Work as a class. Brainstorm a list of features you think the examiner will be looking for in your writing.

> • *Sentences with full stops and . . .*
> • *Paragraphs*
> • *Interesting vocabulary*

14.1 2 Work as a class. Read the question below. Then see together how to ask five questions that will make sure you understand what you have to write.

> A new Youth Club is going to be opened in your area. There is enough money to run the Youth Club on three evenings from 7.30pm to 10.00pm and £1000 to buy some new equipment.
>
> Year 9 students are being asked to send letters advising the Youth Service about how the youth club should be run and what it should offer.
>
> **Write your letter explaining which evenings the club should be open and what it should be like so that you and your friends will enjoy it.**

1 Ask: **What type of text am I being asked to write?** *An informal letter*

2 Ask: **Who is it for?** *The youth service*

3 Ask: **What is its purpose?** *To explain what would make a good youth club.*

4 Ask: **What information does it have to have in it?** *Which three evenings it should be open, what equipment it should have, how it should be run so my friends and I will use it.*

5 Ask: **How formal does the writing have to be?** *Not as formal as a job application but not chatty either. I'll use standard English.*

3 Work in pairs. Use the five questions opposite to work out what you have to do when you answer the question below.

> Your school wants to become more active in recycling. You have been asked to write an article for your school magazine about how students can help to recycle waste. Talk about recycling:
> * paper
> * bottles
> * drink cans.

4 Work on your own. Use the five questions opposite to work out what you have to do when you answer the question below.

> You have been asked to write a formal report for your Headteacher and Governors about how easy it is for students in wheelchairs to use the facilities in your school. You should make sure you consider how easy it is for these students to:
> * arrive at and leave school
> * attend and take part in different types of lessons
> * use sports and leisure equipment
> * use the canteen and toilets.

5 Work in pairs. Do not look back at your work. Make a list of the five questions that will make sure you understand what you have to write. Make sure that you both know them.

14.2

Using a planning frame

This section will help you to:
• use a planning frame

1 Work as a class. Talk about why you need to plan a piece of writing.

14.2 2 Work as a class. In the test you will be given a planning frame to use. Read the example opposite and the labels to see how to use a planning frame.

14.3 3 Work in pairs. Decide together how to fill in the planning frame below. Each of you should fill in your own copy.

Your friend has sent you an e-mail explaining that her younger brother is being very annoying because:
• he borrows her things without asking and has broken some of them
• he doesn't leave her friends in peace when they come round to see her
• she has to babysit for him at weekends when she wants to go out.
She wants your advice on how she can sort things out.
Write her an e-mail giving her advice.
First use the planning frame below to organise your ideas.

Your friend's name:	Her brother's name:
How to sort out the first problem	
How to sort out the second problem	
How to sort out the third problem	
Advice words and phrases you can use	
How the e-mail begins	How the e-mail ends

4 Work on your own. Write your answer using your planning frame.

5 Work as a class. How did your planning frame help you write your answer?

Using a planning frame

Should students be paid to stay on at school?

Write a conversation where two characters discuss this question.
One of them must be in favour of the idea. The other must be against it.
Make their arguments as persuasive as possible. Present the conversation
as a drama script.

Use the planning frame below to help you organise your ideas.

First person – believes students should be paid to stay on at school.	Second person – believes students should **not** be paid to stay on at school.
Name *Kirsty Smith*	Name *Olivia Godfrey*
What sort of person is s/he? *Very down to earth, not well off.* How will you show this? *Speaks in non-standard English, uses slang. Talks about what it's like to be poor.*	What sort of person is s/he? *Wealthy – can't imagine what it's like not to be rich.* How will you show this? *Speaks in standard English. Mentions designer labels, posh shops, etc. Seems to think everyone can afford these.*
Arguments for students being paid • *Parents won't have to support them.* • *Students won't have to give up their studies to earn money.* • *More students will stay on and get better qualifications.* • *Fewer people unemployed.*	Arguments against students being paid • *Costs taxpayers even more money.* • *Students would stay on anyway.* • *Students will just spend money on designer clothes and going out.*

Persuasive words and phrases you can use
Really, only, just, terrible

How conversation will start	Middle of conversation	How conversation ends
Discuss their different points of view.	*Kirsty tells Olivia she has no idea what it's like being poor.*	*Olivia changes her mind and says that students from poorer families should be paid.*

1 Each box gives you clues about what the examiner wants to see in your piece of writing.

2 Work out ideas that you can use when you are writing as you fill in each empty box.

14.3 Creating the right effects

This section will help you to:
- practise creating the effect you are asked for

1 Work as a class. Talk about what each of these words or phrases suggests about the kind of writing the examiner is looking for.

> formal   creepy atmosphere   persuasive
> well supported argument   informal

2 Work as a class. Read the question below and work through the example to see how to build the right effects into your writing. Then read the question again and follow the steps for the other text type needed.

> Your Youth Club is holding a sponsored walk to raise money for poor orphans in Romania. Write a three-paragraph leaflet persuading your friends to take part. In your leaflet you should also say:
> - when the walk will take place
> - where they will walk and how far
> - what they need to bring with them – drinks, sun lotion, hats, etc.

Step 1 Work out what kind of writing is needed

The question says 'persuading' so I need to be persuasive. What sorts of things do I need to do when I write persuasively?

Step 2 Brainstorm what you need to do in that type of writing

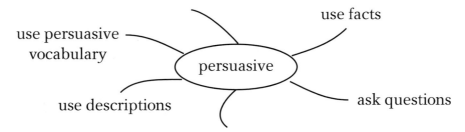

Step 3 Use those effects in your writing

Giving up just one hour of your time on Saturday 18 June could make a huge difference to the lives of poor orphans in Romania. By joining in the Youth Club sponsored walk you could raise money that will buy food, clothes and maybe a few luxuries for these desperate children. Wouldn't you like to make a difference?

3 **Work in pairs. Read the question below, then do these tasks.**

> 1 Brainstorm the sorts of effects you need to use in your answer.
> 2 Write the first paragraph of your answer using those effects.

> The council want to close your local park to build a car park. Write a letter persuading your MP to take action to stop the closure. In your writing you should describe:
> • any birds or animals that use the park
> • people using the park in different ways.

4 **Work on your own. Read the question below, then do these tasks.**

> 1 Decide what sorts of effects you need to use in your answer.
> 2 Write the first paragraph of your answer using those effects.

> Write a formal letter to your local Council persuading them to spend money putting in a new skate park for local teenagers to enjoy. In your letter explain:
> • why a new skate park is needed
> • how it can help keep teenagers fit
> • how it might help reduce problems such as vandalism
> • how having something for teenagers to do would benefit other people in the community.

5 **Work as a class. Share your answers to activity 4. Talk about how you decided which effects to use in your answer.**

14.4 Building your sentences

This section will help you to:
- write in sentences
- use different types of sentences

1 Work as a class. Talk about what you know about writing in sentences. Then brainstorm a list of connectives that you can use in sentences.

and　　*because*　　*in order to*

2 Work as a class. In the test you should take the time to build each sentence carefully. Read 'Litter kills' opposite carefully. Then work through the steps below to see how to write the first sentences of your answer.

Step 1　Think it

Ask:　What do I need to say?

Ask:　How can I say this?

> It's important not to drop litter because litter kills wild animals.

> Do not drop litter — it kills animals.

Step 2　Say it in your head

Ask:　Have I said what I mean?
　　　Does it sound right?
　　　Is this the best way to say it?
　　　Have I shown the examiner that I can use different kinds of sentences?

If the answer to any of these questions is 'No!' go back to Step 1.

> 'Do not drop litter — it kills animals.' said what I meant and sounded OK, but there's probably a better way to say it. I'll try again.

> 'Are you a killer? By dropping just one piece of litter you can kill a wild animal.' That's much better!

Step 3　Write it
- Say each sentence in your head as you write it.
- Start it with a capital letter.
- Remember to use correct punctuation.

Litter kills

There is a serious litter problem in your area which is affecting local wildlife. Your local council has asked you to write a short leaflet to be handed out in the shopping centre to persuade young people not to drop litter. The leaflet will show the picture below.

Write two paragraphs to go on the leaflet. You should:

• explain what harm litter can do

• persuade the reader to take their litter home

• make your paragraphs exciting to read.

3   Work in pairs. Write *four* more persuasive sentences that can be used in the first paragraph of an article explaining what harm dropped litter can do.

4   Work on your own. Write the next paragraph of the article persuading people to take their litter home with them. Take time to work out each sentence carefully.

5   Work as a class.

   1   First work in pairs. Share and mark each other's sentences. Check that each sentence:
      • makes sense
      • begins with a capital letter
      • has the correct punctuation.

   2   Now work as a class. Talk about how you can show the examiner how well you can write different kinds of sentences.

14.5 Writing and linking paragraphs

> **This section will help you to write paragraphs using:**
> - connectives to link points
> - link words to show how your paragraphs follow on

1 Work as a class. Talk about what you know about writing in paragraphs. Then brainstorm a list of link words and phrases that you can use to link sentences.

> *This means ...   In the same way ...   On the other hand ...*

2 Work as a class. In the test you will have to write in paragraphs. Read the example below to remind you about writing in paragraphs.

Should students have to wear school uniform?

Some students at Walton School have raised a petition to ban school uniform. They say that students would like school better if they could choose what to wear. Mrs Keeler, the Headteacher, is in favour of school uniform. She says that students look tidier and have more pride in the school if they wear uniform.

Write three paragraphs discussing whether students should have to wear uniform.

Step 1 Plan what you will write about in each paragraph. Remember you need to begin a new paragraph to write about a different:

- time   • place   • person   • idea

- *Paragraph 1 – explain why having school uniform is a good idea.*
- *Paragraph 2 – explain why it would be better not to have school uniform.*
- *Paragraph 3 – reach my conclusion: school uniform should be banned.*

Step 2 Write one paragraph at a time

- The first sentence must say what the rest of the paragraph is about.
- Use link words to show how an idea follows on from the last one.

Most students have to wear uniform to school and many people think this is a good idea. They argue that wearing school uniform makes students all look the same. This, they say, is a good thing because it means that you can't tell who is rich and who is poor. A uniform also makes it easy for members of the public to tell which school someone belongs to. In the same way, if a student plays truant in school uniform, police or truancy officers can easily spot them and send them back to school.

3 Work on your own. Plan and write the next *two* paragraphs of the argument.

> **1** Begin with a link phrase showing that the second paragraph is about a different point of view.
>
> **2** Use connectives to introduce reasons for your points.
>
> **3** Begin the third paragraph with connectives showing that this is your conclusion.

4 Work on your own. Read the question below, then plan and write the three paragraphs.

Should 14–16-year-olds be allowed to have part-time jobs?

Mrs Green, mother of 15-year-old Nicky, says, 'Working helps teenagers become more responsible and teaches them about working life. Earning their own money makes them much more careful about how they spend it.' Mr Hatchett, Headteacher of Thirsby High School, disagrees. He says, 'Students should be concentrating on their school work, not spending long hours working so that they do not have time to do homework and are tired at school the next day.'

Write three paragraphs discussing whether it is a good idea for 14–16-year-olds to work.

5 Work as a class. Share how you planned and wrote your paragraphs in activity 4. Make a class list of the important things to remember about writing in paragraphs.

15 Analysing *Macbeth*

This unit will help you to:
- understand Shakespeare's play *Macbeth*
- write about the play
- compare the characters in the play
- answer a test question on *Macbeth*

15.1 Comparing characters

This section will help you to:
- compare some of the characters in *Macbeth*
- understand their situation

1 Work as a class. Talk about people you see on television whose characters and behaviour are similar or very different.

 2 Work as a class. Read the information opposite about the characters in *Macbeth* and the notes around them. Then do this work.

> **1** Read about the characters of Macbeth and Lady Macbeth again. Work out together at least *two* ways in which they are alike. Then find *two* ways in which they are different. For example, are they similar or very different in how guilty they feel?
>
> **2** Work out at least *four* sentences to compare the characters of Macbeth and Lady Macbeth. You could start like this:
>
> *Macbeth can be cruel and ...*
> *Lady Macbeth is a powerful personality but ...*

3 Work in pairs. Read about the characters of Macbeth and Banquo again. Write down *one* way that the two men are similar and *two* ways they are different.

> Macbeth and Banquo are both . . .   Macbeth is ... but Banquo ...

4 Work on your own. Write down *three* ways in which Macbeth and Duncan are different.

> Duncan is seen to be ... but Macbeth ...

Duncan: King of Scotland

- good man
- rewards good leaders
- punishes the rebels
- honest
- very trusting
- poor judge of character

1 Will someone like this survive?

Macbeth: one of Duncan's noblemen

- brave leader of army
- ambitious
- wants to be king
- distrusts people
- has doubts
- can be influenced
- weak at times
- becomes cruel • superstitious
- fears good people
- can sometimes feel guilty
- often dishonest • has nightmares
- has hallucinations

2 By witches? By his wife?

Lady Macbeth: Macbeth's wife

- powerful personality
- has very few doubts
- big influence on her husband
- no sense of kindness
- very ambitious
- able to plan murder
- proud of being ruthless
- ends up full of guilt

3 Like her husband.

Banquo: another of Duncan's noblemen

- can be trusted
- not very superstitious
- is not ambitious to be king
- leader of army

4 With Macbeth.

 15.2 **5**

Work as a class.

1 Compare what you have written about Macbeth and Banquo and about Macbeth and Duncan.

2 What do you think might happen to these characters in the play?

15.2

The whole story

> **This section will help you to:**
> - find out what happens in *Macbeth*
> - write about the play
> - talk about what kind of play it is

1 Work as a class. Read the information in the box, then answer the question below.

> **Background information**
>
> *Macbeth* was written in 1606, when England had a new king, James the First. The king, who was Scottish, was very superstitious and had even written a book about witches. His position as king was not very certain and he worried about people plotting to murder him.

1 Imagine you are Shakespeare in 1606. You are writing *Macbeth* to please and interest the king. Which of these things would you put in your play?

> - witches
> - false friends
> - animals
> - a good king
> - nightmares
> - good defeating evil
> - love scenes
> - a king's murder
> - the dangers of superstition
> - battles
> - Scottish scenery

2 Work as a class. Read the picture strip that tells the story of *Macbeth*. Then complete the paragraph at the top of page 167.

Macbeth and Banquo have won a battle for Duncan. They are riding home. Witches appear.

2 A nobleman brings news.

Macbeth, the king has made you Thane of Cawdor. The old thane will be put to death as a traitor.

3 Perhaps I can also be king.

Witches are not to be trusted.

So the witches were right!

4 Duncan announces that his son Malcolm will become king when he dies.

Macbeth writes to his wife about all that has happened. She thinks immediately about murder.

5 Duncan comes to stay the night at Macbeth's castle. Lady Macbeth does not intend him to leave alive.

6 No, I will do it.

Are you afraid?

Macbeth has doubts about killing the king.

7 Macbeth stabs the sleeping king. He is terrified by what he has done.

Lady Macbeth takes the daggers back. She wipes blood on the drugged servants who should have been protecting Duncan.

8 Duncan's murder is discovered by Macduff, a loyal soldier.

O horror!

And then Macbeth kills the two blood-stained servants.

9 Macbeth becomes king. Duncan's sons run for their lives. They fear that whoever killed their father will murder them.

10 Banquo guesses the truth about his friend Macbeth.

He may be king but I fear he is also a murderer.

Macbeth then has Banquo killed because the witches said his descendants would be kings. Banquo's son escapes.

11 Macbeth's great banquet is ruined by a ghost only he can see.

You cannot say I did it!

Lady Macbeth sends the noble guests home before Macbeth says something that reveals the truth.

12 Macbeth returns to the witches. They show him four things.

a

Beware Macduff.

A soldier's head.

b

No one born of woman can harm Macbeth.

A baby covered in blood.

c

Macbeth will not be beaten until Birnan Wood comes to Dunsinane

A child with a tree.

d

Eight kings – all from Banquo's family.

13 Lady Macbeth sleepwalks. She talks about blood and murder.

Here's the smell of blood still.

Her doctor watches but can do nothing.

14 Malcolm and Macduff's army cut down branches from Birnan Wood. They use them to hide their numbers from Macbeth as they march on Dunsinane.

This is what the witches said.

16 The battle begins. Macbeth finds out that Macduff was taken from his mother's womb before birth.

Die, hell-hound!

15

Out, out, brief candle!

Lady Macbeth is found dead. Macbeth reacts by saying how life seems like a useless crawl towards the grave.

Macbeth is killed and Malcolm, Duncan's son, is crowned king.

1 Look back at pictures 1–3. Copy and complete this paragraph.

When _____ and Banquo meet the witches at the start of the play, they are riding back from _____ . The witches make _____ to both of them. The news that Macbeth is to be _____ fulfils one of the witches' promises. Macbeth shows a _____ in the witches and hopes that _____ . However, Banquo is less _____ . He senses that the witches _____ .

3 **Work in pairs on pictures 4–7. Copy and complete this paragraph.**

When Lady Macbeth reads her husband's _____ her thoughts turn to _____ . Macbeth thinks about murder too but he is not as _____ . Macbeth feels _____ about killing Duncan when he is a guest. Lady Macbeth tells her husband that he is _____ . Eventually Macbeth _____ to the murder. After he has stabbed the king, Macbeth is _____ by what he has done. Lady Macbeth is much more _____ and makes it look as if the servants have killed the king.

4 **Work on your own on pictures 8–16. Copy and complete these paragraphs.**

One killing leads to another and Macbeth soon kills the servants and has _____ murdered. The murder returns to haunt him – _____ appears to Macbeth at _____ . No one else _____ . Once again Lady Macbeth appears to be _____ than her husband.

Macbeth goes back to see the witches, who help to give him confidence. However, Lady Macbeth's strength now starts to _____ . She begins to sleepwalk, talking about _____ and murder. She _____ before the final battle. Macbeth reacts by saying how life is _____ . Macbeth _____ in battle, and _____ becomes king.

5 **Work as a class. Discuss some of your answers to the questions above. Talk about what sort of play *Macbeth* seems to be.**

15.3 Beginning and end

This section will help you to:
- understand two parts of the play *Macbeth*
- try out different ways of playing scenes
- get across the atmosphere in performance

1 Work as a class. Answer these questions.

1 What have you learned so far about Macbeth, Lady Macbeth and Duncan?

2 What type of actor would you choose to play each of these parts?

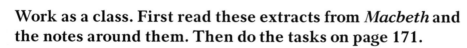

Macbeth should be played by someone ... . A good choice would be ...

2 Work as a class. First read these extracts from *Macbeth* and the notes around them. Then do the tasks on page 171.

A

At the end of Act 1, the king comes to Macbeth's castle.
DUNCAN: This castle hath a pleasant seat; the air
Nimbly and sweetly recommends itself
Unto our gentle senses.

1 He thinks the castle is in a nice place and the air smells good.

Lady Macbeth already has murder in mind but welcomes him.
LADY MACBETH: All our service,
5   In every point twice done, and then done double,
Were poor and single business to contend
Against those honours deep and broad wherewith
Your Majesty loads our house.

2 She's saying that she can't match the king in being generous.

B

At the start of the next scene, Macbeth is alone.

MACBETH: If it were done, when 'tis done, then 'twere well
It were done quickly …
But in these cases … we but teach
Bloody instructions, which being taught return
5   To plague th' inventor …
           … He's here **in double trust**:
First, as I am his kinsman and his subject,
Strong both against the deed; then, as his host …

Then Lady Macbeth joins him.

MACBETH: We will proceed no further in this business.
10   He hath honoured me of late; and I have **bought**
Golden opinions from all sorts of people …

LADY MACBETH: Was the hope drunk
Wherein you dressed yourself? … Art thou afeard …
       … I have given suck, and know
15   How tender 'tis to love the babe that milks me –
I would while it was smiling in my face
Have plucked my nipple from his boneless gums,
And dashed the brains out, had I so sworn as you
Have done to this.

20 MACBETH: If we should fail?

LADY MACBETH: We fail?
But screw your courage to the sticking-place,
And we'll not fail.

> **in double trust** – there are two reasons for not killing him
> **bought** – got

C

Much later, in Act 5, things are very different. The scene starts with Lady Macbeth sleepwalking. Her servant or gentlewoman has been waiting with a doctor, and Lady Macbeth appears carrying a candle.

DOCTOR: You see her eyes are open.

GENTLEWOMAN: Ay but their sense are shut.

DOCTOR: What is it she does now? Look how she rubs her hands.

GENTLEWOMAN: It is an **accustomed** action with her, to seem thus
5   washing her hands. I have known her continue in this a quarter of an hour.

> **accustomed** – usual

LADY MACBETH: Yet here's a spot.

DOCTOR: Hark! She speaks. I will set down what comes from her, to satisfy my remembrance the more strongly.

LADY MACBETH: Out damned spot, out I say! One, two; why then 'tis
10 time to do't. Hell is murky. Fie my lord, fie! A soldier, and afeard? What need we fear who knows it, when none can **call our power to account**? Yet who would have thought the old man to have had so much blood in him?

call our power to account – challenge us

D

While Lady Macbeth is cursed by dreams, Macbeth prepares for battle. The witches' promises seem to have given him strength.

MACBETH: Bring me no more reports, let them fly all.
    Till Birnam wood remove to Dunsinane,
    I cannot taint with fear.

A servant enters. He is scared to tell Macbeth that he has seen some ten thousand English soldiers. Macbeth scorns his fear.

MACBETH: Go prick thy face, and over-red thy fear,
5   Thou lily-livered boy.

3 He is saying: Go and stab yourself, that will bring some colour to your cheeks, you coward.

At the same time, Macbeth is beginning to sound tired of life.

MACBETH: I have lived long enough. My way of life
    Is fallen into the sear.

Is fallen into the sear – has dried up, is pointless
skirr – search

Macbeth may be tired, but the doubts he had earlier about taking violent action have gone.

MACBETH: Send out more horses, **skirr** the country round;
Hang those that talk of fear. Give me mine armour.

1 Look back at what Duncan says in extract **A**. Is he enthusiastic, foolish or just innocent? Try different ways of saying his lines.

2 Look at how Lady Macbeth welcomes Duncan in extract **A**. How will you make her sound convincing? Do you want to give a hint of her wickedness? Try different ways of saying her lines.

3 Read the speech where Macbeth is alone (extract **B**, lines 1–8). What are his doubts about murdering Duncan?

3 **Work in pairs. Look at what Macbeth and Lady Macbeth say to each other (extract B, lines 9–23).**

1 How weak should Macbeth sound?

2 How forceful should Lady Macbeth be? Should she be loud or quiet? Try different ways of saying her lines.

4 **Work in pairs. Look at what Lady Macbeth says when she is sleepwalking in extract C.**

1 Is Lady Macbeth angry, troubled, guilty or all three?

2 Take it in turns to perform the speech for the other person. Try it in at least *two* different ways each. Work on your performances until you are doing them as well as possible.

15.4 **5** **Work in fours. You are going to perform the whole of the sleepwalking scene (extract C).**

1 Agree who will be the director and who will be Lady Macbeth, the doctor and the servant (gentlewoman).

2 Now perform the scene. Try it in different ways in order to create a real sense of tension.

3 When you have practised, perform your versions for the class. What works well?

Comparisons

This section will help you to:
- write formally about *Macbeth*
- use quotations to back up opinions

1 Work as a class. What have you learned so far about Macbeth and Lady Macbeth? Talk about:

- what they are like at the start of the play
- what they do
- what they are like at the end of the play.

2 Work as a class. You are going to write *four* paragraphs which show the differences between Macbeth and Lady Macbeth. Remember to use formal language.

1 Complete this paragraph together. Then make your own copy.

1 nerves? bad feelings? doubts and fears?

3 scared silly? troubled? fazed?

The changes that occur to Macbeth and Lady Macbeth are central to what happens in Shakespeare's play. In the first act, it appears to be Macbeth who is experiencing _____ while Lady Macbeth is _____ for murder. Macbeth is _____ by what might happen 'if we fail'. His wife has no such doubts. She tells him to 'screw your courage _____' and to trust that they will succeed.

2 enthusiastic? willing and prepared?

4 Look at line 22 of extract **B**.

15.5 **3**

Work in pairs to complete this second paragraph. Write up your own copy of your answer.

> Macbeth wants to be king. He has ambition. However, he also _____ people's 'Golden opinions' of himself for a time. He does not want to take the risk that the 'Bloody instructions' of a murder will return to _____ . Lady Macbeth appears to be much _____ . She declares she would have been willing to have 'dashed _____ ' of her own baby rather than give up _____ .

1 fancies hearing? wants to enjoy?

2 haunt him? give him heartache?

3 more relaxed? trickier? stronger?

4 Look at line 18 of extract **B**.

5 being in charge? the chance of the crown?

15.5 **4**

Work on your own to copy and complete the third and fourth paragraphs.

> By the end of the play, the roles are _____ .
> Lady Macbeth is troubled by the kind of _____ that affected Macbeth earlier in the play. She sleepwalks and sees the blood of the murders again. Her gentlewoman tells the doctor that she washes her hands for up to 'a quarter _____ '. No matter how hard she tries, she feels that she will never be free from _____ .
>
> In contrast, Macbeth has become the kind of soldier who will _____ . The witches' promise has made him _____ . When a frightened servant appears to tell him about ten thousand English soldiers, he calls him 'a lily-_____ ,' a coward. Although he is not afraid, Macbeth is clearly _____ . Everything seems withered. He may have power but it has become pointless to him.

1 back to front? reversed? switched?

2 dreams? fantasies? nightmares?

3 Look at line 5 of extract **C**.

4 the washing? her troubles? the blood?

5 kill like crazy? take on any challenge?

6 fearless? ready to fight?

7 Look at line 7 of extract **D**.

8 cheesed off? tired of life? done in?

5 **Work as a class.**

1 Listen to a selection of your answers.

2 Talk about why you would choose formal English for writing like this.

Answering a test question on *Macbeth*

This section will help you to:
- revise the characters of Macbeth and Lady Macbeth
- understand an example of a test question
- write an answer to the test question

 Work as a class. You are going to revise the characters of Macbeth and Lady Macbeth.

1 First work in pairs. Look at the mixed-up list of words and phrases to describe Macbeth and Lady Macbeth. Put each word or phrase into the correct column of a chart like the one below.

- ambitious
- very ambitious
- loyal
- wants to be king
- fears good people
- weak at times
- often dishonest
- becomes cruel
- superstitious
- can sometimes feel guilty
- has doubts
- big influence on husband
- can be influenced
- no sense of kindness
- able to plan murder
- proud of being ruthless
- ends up full of guilt
- has very few doubts
- powerful personality

Macbeth	Lady Macbeth
ambitious	very ambitious

2 Now work as a class. Read the question below, then complete these tasks.

   a Identify the key words in the question which help you understand what you are being asked to do.

   b What are the words in *italics* asking you to do?

   c Discuss how you would go about answering the question.

> **What impressions might an audience get of Macbeth from the different ways he speaks and behaves in the extracts on pages 176–177?**
>
> *Support your ideas by referring to the extracts which are printed on pages 176–177.*

 2 Work as a class. Justin, a Year 9 student, has made a plan for the first part of his answer to the question above, using extracts A and B from Act 1. Look at the plan and read the labels around it. Then talk about how this plan would help you to answer the question.

1 You are not given a planning frame in the test, but doing a plan will help you to write better.

Macbeth's character at the end of Act 1		
Point	Evidence	Explanation
Loyal	'… He's here in double trust:… I am his kinsman and his subject … then, as his host …'	Macbeth can't kill someone who is a family member and guest.
Can sometimes feel guilty	'We will proceed no further in this business'	He has thought about it and doesn't want to kill King Duncan any more.

2 In this column, points about character and behaviour are noted.

3 In this column, words from the text are noted which prove your point.

4 A brief explanation of the point and evidence is noted here.

A

At the end of Act 1, the king comes to Macbeth's castle.

DUNCAN: This castle hath a pleasant seat; the air
        Nimbly and sweetly recommends itself
        Unto our gentle senses.

Lady Macbeth already has murder in mind but welcomes him.

LADY MACBETH: All our service,
5   In every point twice done, and then done double,
        Were poor and single business to contend
        Against those honours deep and broad wherewith
        Your Majesty loads our house.

B

At the start of the next scene, Macbeth is alone.

MACBETH: If it were done, when 'tis done, then 'twere well
        It were done quickly …
        But in these cases … we but teach
        Bloody instructions, which being taught return
5   To plague th' inventor …
            … He's here in double trust:
        First, as I am his kinsman and his subject,
        Strong both against the deed; then, as his host …

Lady Macbeth joins him.

MACBETH: We will proceed no further in this business.
10   He hath honoured me of late; and I have bought
        Golden opinions from all sorts of people …

LADY MACBETH: Was the hope drunk
        Wherein you dressed yourself? … Art thou afeard …
            … I have given suck, and know
15   How tender 'tis to love the babe that milks me –
        I would while it was smiling in my face
        Have plucked my nipple from his boneless gums,
        And dashed the brains out, had I so sworn as you
        Have done to this.

20 MACBETH: If we should fail?

LADY MACBETH: We fail?
        But screw your courage to the sticking-place,
        And we'll not fail.

C

Lady Macbeth appears carrying a candle.

DOCTOR: You see her eyes are open.

GENTLEWOMAN: Ay but their sense are shut.

DOCTOR: What is it she does now? Look how she rubs her hands.

GENTLEWOMAN: It is an accustomed action with her, to seem thus
5   washing her hands. I have known her continue in this a quarter of an hour.

LADY MACBETH: Yet here's a spot.

DOCTOR: Hark! She speaks. I will set down what comes from her, to
satisfy my remembrance the more strongly.

LADY MACBETH: Out damned spot, out I say! One, two; why then 'tis
10   time to do't. Hell is murky. Fie my lord, fie! A soldier, and afeard? What
need we fear who knows it, when none can call our power to account? Yet
who would have thought the old man to have had so much blood in him?

D

Macbeth is preparing for battle.

MACBETH: Bring me no more reports, let them fly all.
   Till Birnam wood remove to Dunsinane,
   I cannot taint with fear.

A servant enters.

MACBETH: Go prick thy face, and over-red thy fear,
5   Thou lily-livered boy.

At the same time, Macbeth is beginning to sound tired of life.

MACBETH: I have lived long enough. My way of life
   Is fallen into the sear.

*Macbeth may be tired, but the doubts he had earlier about taking violent
action have gone.*

MACBETH: Send out more horses, skirr the country round;
Hang those that talk of fear. Give me mine armour.

3 Work as a pair.

> **1** Complete the plan below for the character of Macbeth in Act 5 (extracts **C** and **D**). First put in the missing explanation, then add one more point with evidence and explanation. Use Justin's plan from page 175 to help you. Make sure you each make a copy of your plan.
>
> **2** Share your work with the class.

Macbeth's character at the end of Act 5		
Point	Evidence	Explanation
Superstitious	'Till Birnam wood remove to Dunsinane, I cannot taint with fear'	

4 Work as a class. Read the first paragraph opposite of Justin's answer and look at the labels around it. Then complete these tasks.

> **1 a** Look at the second paragraph. Identify the point, evidence and explanation.
>
> **b** How did the plan help Justin to write these two paragraphs?
>
> **c** What has Justin added that is not in the plan?
>
> **2** Now work on your own. Using your plan, write two paragraphs to describe what Macbeth is like in Act 5. Use Justin's paragraphs to help you.

5 Work as a class.

> **1** First work on your own to check the paragraphs you have written.
>
> **a** Read your paragraphs.
>
> - Have you organised your plan into a clear 'point, evidence, explanation' paragraph?
> - Have you used quotation marks around the words from the play (the evidence)?
>
> **b** Read through your paragraphs again. Do they answer the question on page 175?
>
> **2** Now share your paragraphs with the class. Talk about how making a plan helped you to write a good answer.

Macbeth's character at the end of Act 1		
Point	Evidence	Explanation
Loyal	'... He's here in double trust:... I am his kinsman and his subject ... then, as his host ...'	Macbeth can't kill someone who is a family member and guest.
Can sometimes feel guilty	'We will proceed no further in this business'	He has thought about it and doesn't want to kill King Duncan any more.

1 Justin has added some information about what is happening.

3 This is the evidence from the plan.

2 This is the point from the plan.

4 This is the explanation from the plan.

At the end of Act 1, Macbeth is speaking his thoughts aloud. He is having doubts about killing King Duncan. He shows that he is loyal to the king. He says, 'He's here in double trust:... I am his kinsman and his subject ... then, as his host ...'. Even though he wants to be king, he knows that it is wrong to kill someone in his family who is a guest in his castle.

5

He shows these doubts again when he sees Lady Macbeth. He tells her, 'We will proceed no further in this business.' He has thought about all the reasons why he should not kill Duncan and decided that he doesn't want to do it any more.

10

Macbeth has doubts about killing the king.

16 Dictionaries and spellcheckers

This unit will help you to:
- use a dictionary or a computer spellchecker
- choose the form of the word that you need (verb, noun, etc.)
- work out which word you need from a spellchecker list

This will help you to: spell words from different subjects

---

1 When you look up a word in a dictionary, you often find more information than you need. Look at the dictionary entry below and the labels around it.

1 This shows how to pronounce the word. The part in **bold** is *stressed* (said more clearly).

object (*say* **ob**-jekt) *noun*
  1. anything which can be seen, touched or perceived by any of the senses.
  2. a person or thing to which attention, thought, action, etc. is directed: a) 'the unhappy child was an *object* of pity'; b) the *object* of the meeting is to elect a president'.
object (*say* ob-**jekt**) *verb*
  to disapprove of, dislike, feel or argue against: 'I *object* to your coming in without knocking first'.
Word Family: **objector**, *noun*, a person who objects; **objectify** (**objectified**, **objectifying**), *verb*, a) to make objective, b) to present as an object.
[Latin *objectus* thrown in the way]

2 The type of word (noun, verb) this definition is for.

3 There are two meanings for this word.

4 Examples are given to help you understand the meaning.

5 Other words connected to the main word are given.

6 This shows what language the word came into English from.

---

2 Work with a partner. Practise pronouncing 'object' in the two ways given in the dictionary entry.

---

3 Read the sentences below. Decide which definition of the word 'object' you need in each one. Hint: first decide what type of word it is.

A
I don't like hockey! What's the point of chasing a small round object all afternoon?

B
I don't usually object, but it's snowing today!

C
I thought the object of doing sport was to get fit, not to freeze to death!

---

4 Now read the dictionary entry again. Write all the words in bold in the correct column of a table like the one below.

Word	Noun	Verb
object	*object*	

Using a computer spellchecker

When you use a computer to write a text, you can use the spellchecker to check your spellings. To check one word, highlight the word and click on the spellchecker icon. Otherwise use the spellchecker when you have completed your text.

The spellchecker will usually offer several possible words based on the way you have spelt the word. To work out which is the correct word for your sentence, think about what would make sense.

5 A student wrote the sentences below and used a spellchecker to check them. You can see the results below. Choose the most suitable suggested words and rewrite the sentences.

A The boys ate the **entrir** cake in front of the **entrir** to the house.
B The driver had to make a **dicishon** to follow the **divesin**.
C Our local team is about to **entrir** the second **divesin**.
D 'And now John **divesin** and makes a perfect **entrir** into the water.'

Not in dictionary	Not in dictionary	Not in dictionary
Divesin	Dicishon	Entrir
Suggestions	**Suggestions**	**Suggestions**
Dives in	Decision	Entire
Divesting	Division	Enter
Division	Dickson	Entry
Diversion	Divisions	Enterer
Devising		Entree
		Entrap

17 Checking your work for spelling errors

In this unit you will learn to:
- check your work
- notice and correct your spelling errors

There are several reasons why it is hard to check your own work for errors. You are going to learn some strategies for dealing with them.

1 Your handwriting is unclear, so you can't see how you have spelt the difficult word

We <u>tastid</u> four <u>difrent</u> types of food with our eyes closed. We had to <u>identiffy</u> which taste buds could taste the <u>difrent</u> types of food (<u>sower</u>, sweet, salt and <u>biter</u>).

Strategy

1   Print each word clearly (not joined up) as it has been spelt in the extract.
2   Check whether your printed version looks right.
3   If you are not sure, use a dictionary to check the spelling.

1   **Use the strategy to correct the errors underlined in the sentences above.**

2 The word is a homophone

Some words sound the same when you say them but have different spellings and meanings. They are called *homophones*. It can be hard to know which spelling to use. Look at these examples of homophones.

here / hear   where / wear   brake / break

Strategy

Find a way to remember one of the spellings that is connected to the meaning of the word. If that isn't the meaning you need, you probably need the other spelling. Look at these two examples.

- 'I hear with my ear' links the spelling of this type of 'hear' with the spelling of 'ear'.

- If you have a mental picture of the word 'break' broken into two, you will remember to use that spelling to mean to break or smash something.

bre)(ak

2 **Work with a partner. Work out a clever way to remember one word in each of these pairs of homophones.**

sale / sail	pain / pane	plain / plane	through / threw	been / bean

3 It is a word that you always get wrong

Like most people, you may always get a few words wrong. It is hard to spot that they are wrong in your writing.

Strategy

If these are words you often need, you should:

- learn them using strategies from the list below
- keep a list of them, written clearly and correctly.

> - Strategy 1: Break the word into syllables
> - Strategy 2: Sound the word out
> - Strategy 3: Find and remember the tricky part
> - Strategy 4: Find another word you can spell that sounds similar
> - Strategy 5: Think of a catchy way to remember the spelling
> - Strategy 6: Look, say, cover, write and check

3 **The words below are often spelt incorrectly. Choose *three* words that you find hard to remember. Use the best strategy from the list above to help you learn each one.**

author	unnecessary	separate	accommodation
February	respiration	scientific	experiment

Vowels you can't hear

e.g. page 47: memory

When people speak they say some syllables clearly. Other syllables are difficult to hear because they are said quickly or not at all. For example, the word *myst/e/ry* often sounds like *mystry* because the 'e' is not said.

Words that end with '-ry' often have a vowel you can't hear, for example: *dictionary, mystery, history*

1 These words all have a vowel you can't hear before '-ry'. Write each word down, then say it out loud. Underline the vowel you can't hear.

jewellery	dictionary	factory	category	ordinary
secretary	solitary	secondary	conservatory	planetary
mystery	cemetery	history	observatory	boundary

2 Now sort the words above into three groups according to the vowel you can't hear. Fill in a table like the one below.

'a'	'e'	'o'
secretary	jewellery	

3 Use your table to help you decide which vowel you can't hear is the most common. Which is the least common?

4 To spell a word with a vowel you can't hear, write it and see if it looks right.

1 Cover the top of this page with a piece of paper. Choose '-ary', '-ery' or '-ory' to complete each of these words. Does the word look right?

second_____ conservat_____ myst_____ bound_____ hist_____

ordin_____ categ_____ cemet_____ solit_____ diction_____

2 Now use the words in the box above to check your words. Learn the correct spellings for any words you got wrong. (Hint: say all the syllables in the word, stressing the vowel you can't hear, to help you remember that it is there: *myst/e/ry*)

19 Words ending in '-ar', '-er' and '-or'

e.g. page 48:
corridor,
power

This unit will help you to:
- learn the most common ways to spell the 'er' sound at the end of a word

This will help you to spell words such as: shoulder, grammar, weather, author, terror

The 'er' sound at the end of words can be spelled in three different ways:
weather, author, mirror, motor, calendar

1 **Find *fourteen* words in this text which have the 'er' sound at the end.**

> My father is a faster driver than my brother, even though he is older. One frosty winter's morning in December, he was on his regular road to town when a police officer stopped him for speeding. He said he was a doctor on his way to deliver a visitor's baby, although he was really an author rushing a book to his publisher!

2 **Sort the words into three groups. Write them in a table like the one below.**

ar	er	or	
	father	author	

3 **Add *two* extra words to each group.** Hint: there are words on this page that might help you.

4 **Use your table to help you answer these questions.**

1 Which spelling of the 'er' sound is the most common?
2 How do you spell the 'er' sound at the end of the months?
3 How do you spell the 'er' sound at the end of comparative adjectives (taller, greater)?

5 **Choose *four* words from activity 2. Choose a strategy from page 183 to help you learn to spell them. Remember: if you need a word often, you should learn how to spell it.**

20 Prefixes

e.g. page 65:
radiotherapy,
chemotherapy

This unit will help you to:
- understand the meanings of some common prefixes
- recognise other prefixes and predict their meaning

This will help you to spell words such as: audience, aerodynamics microscopic, primary

1 **Words with the prefixes 'audi-', 'aero-', 'micro-' and 'prim-' are used in many of the subjects you study.** Look at the table below to see what they mean and how they are used.

Prefix	audi-	aero-	micro-	prim-
Meaning	hear	air	small	first
Word from science	audible	aerodynamics	microscope	primate
Word from PE		aerobics		
Word from geography		aerial	microclimate	primary source

2 **Sort these words according to their prefixes. Write them in a table like the one below.**

audition	primrose	microphone	auditorium
aeronaut	primary	micrometer	aerodrome

audi-	aero-	micro-	prim-

3 **Discuss with a partner what the words in the table mean.** The meanings of the prefixes should help you. Use a dictionary to check your answers.

4 **Use a dictionary to find another word with each of the prefixes 'audi-', 'aero-', 'micro-' and 'prim-'. Add them to your table.**

5 **Now you are going to look at words with the prefixes 'pre-', 'contra-' and 'inter-'.** Copy and complete the table below.

1 Look up 'predict' and 'interface' in a dictionary to find out what they mean.
2 Try to work out what the prefixes 'pre-' and 'contra-' mean.
3 Find one more word with each prefix.

Prefix	pre-	contra-	inter-
Meaning of prefix			between
Example	predict	contradict	interface
Meaning of word		speak against	
New word			

21 Suffixes: '-able' and '-ible'

This unit will help you to:
• learn the main spelling rules when you add suffixes '-able' and '-ible'

This will help you to spell words such as:
terrible, disposable, responsible, enjoyable

'-able' or '-ible'?

In words such as 'edible' and 'enjoyable', the endings sound the same. These hints might help you:

• '-able' is used more often than '-ible'.
• Remove the ending from the word. If you are left with a whole word, the ending is '-able'. Otherwise, it could be either ending.

1 **Read the text below. Use the hints above to add suffix '-able' or '-ible' to complete each word.**

> I've damaged my Mum's best jug. It's got a notice_____ chip, and it's not replace_____ . Even if it's repair_____ , will it be afford_____ ?
> I knew it was break_____ – perhaps it wasn't a suit_____ football!

2 **Read the text below. Pick out *ten* words ending in '-able' or '-ible'. Copy them into two separate boxes.**

> It is probable that global warming is irreversible. There are reliable reports of a measurable hole in the ozone layer, and its growth seems unstoppable. Because oil is not renewable it would be sensible to use less fuel, but we seem incapable of this. The future is unpredictable, but it is impossible not to feel gloomy.

3 **Fill the gaps in this text. Use the word or word stem in brackets with '-able' or '-ible'.** Hint: look back over this page if you need help.

> My dad's car is just not _____ (rely). It's quite _____ (cap-) of running well, but it isn't _____ (predict). On a good day, it's _____ (poss-) to drive it for miles, but then the next day it's _____ (prob-) that it won't go at all. It makes a _____ (terr-) noise and gives off _____ (horr-) black smoke. I think it's really only _____ (suit) for scrap!

22 Suffixes: '-en', '-ify', '-ise'

e.g. page 147:
compromise

This unit will help you to:
- understand how the meaning of words change when you add the suffixes '-en', '-ify', '-ise'
- learn the main rules for adding these suffixes

This will help you to spell words such as: lengthen, notify, apologise

Some nouns (n) and adjectives (adj) become verbs (v) when you add the suffixes '-en', '-ify', '-ise':

length (n) ⟶ lengthen (v); note (n) ⟶ notify (v); apology (n) ⟶ apologise (v)

1 **Change these nouns and adjectives to verbs by adding the correct suffix.**
Check in the dictionary if you are not sure.

Nouns and adjectives	Suffixes	Verbs
pure (adj)		purify
deep (adj)	-en	
class (n)		
dead (adj)	-ify	
real (adj)		
patron (n)	-ise	
apology (n)		

Spelling rules

Rule A: Nouns or adjectives ending in 'e' or 'y'	Drop the 'e' and add the suffix: *simple ⟶ simplify; summary ⟶ summarise*
Rule B: Most other nouns and adjectives	Add the suffix: *real ⟶ realise; solid ⟶ solidify*

2 **Sort the words in the table into lists A and B, following the spelling rules above.**

3 **Read the sentences below. Use the spelling rules to turn the words in brackets into verbs. Then re-read each sentence to check that it makes sense.**

1 The camper used a filter to _____ (pure) the water.
2 The builders brought steel rods to _____ (strength) the walls.
3 The scientist needed a microscope to _____ (class) the plants.
4 The waiter should _____ (apology) for spilling the soup.

23 Unusual plurals

g. page 151:
ce

This unit will help you to:
- spell the plural forms of nouns that end in 'f' or 'fe':
- spell the plural forms of nouns that don't add 's'

This will help you to spell plurals like: cliffs, halves, children

1 **You are going to learn some new rules for making plurals of nouns. First talk about the three rules you already know. Use these examples to help you:**

church ⟶ churches   body ⟶ bodies   pattern ⟶ patterns

Nouns ending in 'f', 'fe' or 'ff'

Rule A	Words ending in 'ff' – just add 's': *cliff* ⟶ *cliffs*
Rule B	Most words ending in 'f' and 'fe' – just add 's': *chief* ⟶ *chiefs*
Rule C	Some words ending in 'f' and 'fe' – change the 'f' to 'v' and add 'es': *elf* ⟶ *elves*
Hint: Say the plural out loud. You can usually hear if the word has a 'v' sound.

2 **Read the paragraph below. Find *eight* plurals of words ending in 'f', 'fe' or 'ff'. Decide which rule each one follows.**

The bull mastiffs were barking themselves silly. Dan spotted some thieves carrying knives in the yard. Luckily the proofs of his latest book were in two safes in the house. Grabbing his scarves from the shelves by the door, he dashed out.

3 **Now fill the gaps in this paragraph with the plurals of the words in brackets.**

The _____ (mastiff) snapped at the _____' (thief) _____ (calf). Dan's sons and their _____ (wife) joined the chase. The _____ (thief) ran for their _____ (life) towards the barn _____ (roof), but two police _____ (chief) were waiting to put them in _____ (handcuff).

4 **Work out the plurals of the words in the box. Then use the plurals you have made to complete the sentences below.**

child	tooth
sheep	mouse
foot	

1 When young _____ lose their first _____, they put them under their pillows.

2 _____ are much bigger than _____, but they both have four _____ .

189

24 Word families

This unit will help you to:
- use words that you know to help you spell other word

This will help you to spell words like:
sign, signature, signpost
part, particular, participant
infinite, definite

Many words contain a root word or word stem that will help you to spell and understand them.

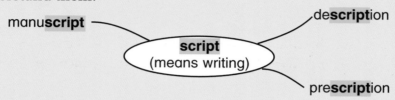

manu**script**

script
(means writing)

de**script**ion

pre**script**ion

Knowing what 'script' means helps you to work out what other words mean. For example:

$$sub + \textbf{script} = sub\textbf{script}$$

means   means   means
'below'   'writing'   'writing placed below the line'

1 **Look at the word web below.**

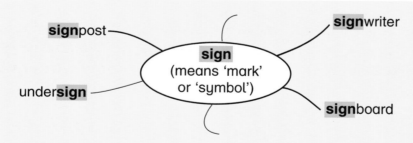

signpost

sign
(means 'mark'
or 'symbol')

signwriter

under**sign**

signboard

1 Use what you know about the meaning of 'sign' to work out what the other *four* words mean. You can use a dictionary to help you.

2 Now use your dictionary to find *two* more words with the root 'sign'.

2 **Look at the words in the box. Then answer the questions below.**

> infinite   definite   finish   final

1 What do the words have in common (the *root stem*)?
2 What is the meaning of the root stem? (Hint: look at the words you already know.)
3 What do 'infinite' and 'definite' mean? Use a dictionary if you need help.

3 **You can build new words by adding prefixes and suffixes to a root word. How many new words can you make which are based on the word 'create'? Use a dictionary to help you.**

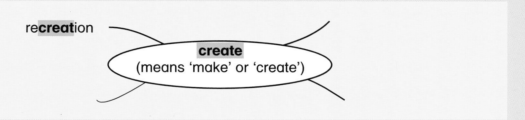

4 **Make a new word web using the root word 'part'. Use a dictionary to help you. Make sure that you know the meanings of the words you make.**

5 **You can also build new words starting from a prefix. Knowing what the prefix means will help you work out what the new words mean. How many new words can you make using the prefix 'inter-'? Use a dictionary to help you.**

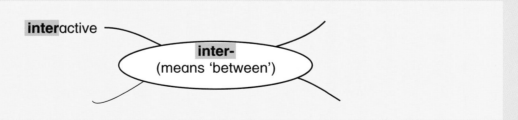

6 **Make a new word web based on the prefix 'mini-'. Use a dictionary to help you. Make sure that you know the meanings of the words you make.**

Heinemann Educational Publishers
Halley Court, Jordan Hill, Oxford, OX2 8EJ
Part of Harcourt Education

Heinemann is the registered trademark of
Harcourt Education Limited

Text © Parts A and B: Jill Baker, Clare Constant, David Kitchen 2003
Text © Part C: Louise Dempsey and Isabel Wright, 2003

The authors and publishers would like to thank Caroline Hannan for her sterling work in the development
of this series which has been warmly appreciated, and David Robinson for acting as our much-valued grammar
consultant. *Per ardua ad astra*

First published 2003

08 07 06 05 04 03
10 9 8 7 6 5 4 3 2 1

British Library Cataloguing in Publication Data is available
from the British Library on request

ISBN 0 435 22686 X

Produced by Bridge Creative Services Limited, Bicester, Oxon
Original illustrations © Harcourt Education Ltd 2003
Illustrated by Andrew Morris: page 5, 12, 13, 163, 164, 165, 166, 168, 169, 170, 174, 179, Nick Schon: page 6, 182,
Serena Curmi: page 8, 79, Kathryn Baker: page 9, 10, 54, 56, 58, 83, 88, 153, 157, 161, Phil Healey: page 15,
John Storey: page 17, 18, Jo Blake: page 20, 35, 37, 42, 124, Paul McCaffrey: page 24, Shelly Revill: page 39, 41, 43,
44, 52, Martin Ursell: page 46, 49, 53, 128, 133, John Storey: page 61, Debbie Boon: page 71, Chris Molan: page 72,
73, 76, Sarah Fisher: page 85, Laura Haddy: page 110, Geoff Ward: page 128, 130, Pantelis Palios: page 151, 189,
Chris Brown: page 159.
Cover design by macdesign ltd
Printed in Spain by Edelvives
Cover photo: ©

Acknowledgements
**Every effort has been made to contact copyright holders of material
reproduced in this book. Any omissions will be rectified in subsequent
printings if notice is given to the publishers.**
'Wanted – A Witch's Cat' by Shelagh McGee. Reprinted with the kind
permission of the author. Extracts from *Stone Cold* by Robert Swindells
(Hamish Hamilton, 1993) Copyright © Robert Swindells, 1993. Reprinted
with permission of Penguin, UK. *Voodoo* by Frederic Browne. Reprinted with
the kind permission of Barry N. Malzberg. Extract from 'Faces' by Dennis
Hamley, from *The Shirt from a Hanged Man's Back* published by Andre
Deutsch. Reprinted with the kind permission of the author. 'Duncan gets
Expelled' by Jackie Kay, from *Two's Company* published by Puffin. Copyright
© Jackie Kay. Reprinted by permission of Peters Fraser & Dunlop on behalf of
Jackie Kay. 'Different' by Joan Poulson, from *Excuses, Excuses* published by
Oxford University Press in 1997. Copyright © Joan Poulson. Reprinted with
the kind permission of the author. 'Dad, Can I Come Home?' by Malorie
Blackman, from *Words Last Forever*. Words Last Forever © 1997 Oneta
Malorie Blackman, Dad Can I Come Home? © 1990 Oneta Malorie
Blackman. Published by Egmont Books Limited, and reproduced with
permission. Extract from *The Red Room* by H. G. Wells, Reprinted with
permission of A. P. Watt Limited on behalf of Literary Executors of Estate of
H. G. Wells. 'Teenage Cancer' from *MIZZ* 445 29/5/02 – 11/6/02. ©
MIZZ/IPC Syndication. Reprinted with permission of IPC Syndication. Jacket
and extracts from *The Little Book of Calm* by Paul Wilson. First published by
Penguin Books Australia Ltd 1996. Copyright © Pearls of Wison, 1996.
Reprinted with permission of Penguin Books Australia Ltd. Jacket and
extracts from *The Little Book of Stress* by Rohan Candappa, published by
Ebury Press. Used by permission of The Random House Group Limited.
Homepage from www.globalgang.org.uk reprinted with the kind permission of
Christian Aid and Paul Fitzgerald (illustrator). Extracts from Save the
Children's Beat Poverty campaign. Reprinted with the kind permission of

Save the Children. Orbit Advert and slogan, reprinted with the kind
permission of The Wrigley Company Limited. Extract from *The Candle House*
by Pauline Fisk, published by Bodley Head. Used by permission of The
Random House Group Limited. Extract from *Ainsley Harriott's Meals in
Minutes* by Ainsley Harriott. Copyright © Ainsley Harriott 1998. Reproduced
by permission of BBC Worldwide Limited. Extract from *The Phantom
Tollbooth* by Norton Juster. Copyright © Norton Juster. Reprinted by
permission of HarperCollins Publishers Limited. Extract from *A Walk in the
Woods* by Bill Bryson published by Black Swan, a division of Transworld
Publishers. © Bill Bryson. All rights reserved. Reprinted with permission of
Transworld Publishers. 'Bird's Eye' slogan *Who cares if you eat well? Birds Eye
cares.* Reprinted with permission of Unilever. Nescafe slogan *Nescafe – the
coffee lover's coffee.* Reprinted by permission of Nestle UK. Maybelline slogan
Maybe she's born with it. Maybe it's Maybelline. Reprinted by permission of
L'Oreal UK Limited. Mars slogan *MARS – pleasure you can't measure.*
Reprinted by permission of Mars UK Ltd. MARS (R) is a registered trademark
of Mars UK Limited Mattel slogan *My Style. My City. My Scene.* Reprinted by
permission of Mattel Press Office. Mr. Muscle slogan *Mr. Muscle – loves the
jobs you hate.* Reprinted by permission of S C Johnson Limited. HSBC slogan
HSBC The world's local bank. Reprinted by permission of HSBC. MORE
TH>N slogan *Don't accept less than MORE TH>N.* Reprinted by permission of
MORE TH>N/Royal Sun Alliance

**The publishers would like to thank the following for permission to
reproduce photographs on the pages noted.**
Cover: Image State (open books, traffic lights); Corbis (keyboard); Inside:
Bloodaxe/Jerry Bauer (Jackie Kay p28); The Sale and Altrincham Messenger
(Joan Poulson p30); PA Photos (Manchester Children's Hospital p66);
Photodisc (football p92); Action Plus/Matthew Clarke (football fan p93);
Corbis/Rob and Sas (family p112); Corbis/Larry Williams (Child p113);
Jeremy Hicks Associates (Ainsley Harriot p147).